Neuropsychological Bases of God Beliefs

Neuropsychological Bases of God Beliefs

MICHAEL A. PERSINGER

PRAEGER

New York
Westport, Connecticut
London

Library of Congress Cataloging-in-Publication Data

Persinger, Michael A.
Neuropsychological bases of God beliefs.

Includes index.
1. Neuropsychology. 2. Psychology, Religious.
3. Experience (Religion) I. Title.
QP360.P458 1987 200'.1'9 87-14689
ISBN 0-275-92648-6 (alk. paper)

Library of Congress Catalog Card Number: 87-14689
ISBN: 0-275-92648-6

First published in 1987

Praeger Publishers, One Madison Avenue, New York, NY 10010
A division of Greenwood Press, Inc.

Printed in the United States of America

The paper used in this book complies with the Permanent Paper Standard issued by the National Information Standards Organization (Z39.48-1984).

P

In order to keep this title in print and available to the academic community, this edition was produced using digital reprint technology in a relatively short print run. This would not have been attainable using traditional methods. Although the cover has been changed from its original appearance, the text remains the same and all materials and methods used still conform to the highest book-making standards.

Contents

List of Figures

Preface

An objective explanation for why people believe in God is not very popular. Like the earlier studies of sex, death, and the origin of humanity, the application of contemporary methods to sacred topics is taboo. Scientists may encounter resistance, ranging from quiet but cordial avoidance to outright physical violence. During the development of the explanation in this text, I have experienced both.

Although there are many reasons for this opposition, two major features are conspicuous. First, the subject matter is extremely sensitive. Since behavioral scientists (the individuals best trained in this particular approach to religion) are themselves human beings, the God Problem involves their own existence as well. It is hard to maintain an analytical insulation between objective and personal significance, especially when the results may indict one's own existence.

The second major reason is that scholars who have written about the God Problem have maintained, often in a contrived manner, a distinction between religious phenomena and all other forms of human behavior. Writers who demand this dichotomy have a clear commitment to the status quo. Their compulsion to write stems from the same source as their personal God Experiences.

An objective understanding of the God Experience is more than just another philosophical pursuit. Reports of meaningful and profound personal relationships with gods, such as Allah, Jehovah, Yahweh, or even the Great Cosmic Whole, are extraordinarily frequent behaviors. One brief episode of the God Experience can change the life of an individual. When embedded within the rules of human culture, a collection of these experiences can form the dynamic core of a religious movement.

In this book, the principles of learning and brain function are applied to the

God Problem. After the introduction, which deals with various dangers of God Experiences and how people with different beliefs will respond to this book, the first component of the explanation is developed. It allows the practitioner to predict the conditions and content of God reports.

Chapters 2 and 3 contain the biological component of the explanation. The primary conclusion is that God Experiences are products of the human brain. When certain portions of the brain are stimulated, God Experiences, tempered by the person's learning history, are evoked. They appear to have emerged within the human species as a means of dealing with the expanded capacity to anticipate aversive events.

God Experiences are predicted to be correlated with transient electrical instabilities within the temporal lobe of the human brain. These temporal lobe transients (TLTs) are normal changes that are precipitated by maturation, personal dilemma, grief, fatigue, and a variety of physiological conditions. Productions of TLTs create an intense sense of meaningfulness, profundity, and conviction.

Specific content of the private behaviors that people label as "the God Experience" reflect both the specific part of the temporal lobe involved and the learning history of the individual. Although dominated by the rich imagery of individual differences, God Experiences contain common themes of "knowing," forced thinking, inner voices, familiarity, and sensations of uplifting movements. In more extreme conditions, God Experiences are associated with personality disorders and epileptic-type hallucinations.

The perceived proof of the God Experience is dependent on each person's belief in his or her own uniqueness. Consequences of this conclusion are outlined in Chapter 4. Because of the tremendous power of the egocentric reference, to which we are all prone, people believe that private experiences are valid measures of certain classes of phenomena, particularly the God Experience.

Chapter 5 deals with the means by which conceptual contradictions are contained within an individual's experience. As long as the tenuous nature of personal proofs can be isolated from the concrete world of public verification, the believer can exist. This separation is maintained by the occasional alterations of memory and by the tendency for people to learn religious behaviors in specific situations. It is also facilitated by seeking peer groups with similar belief systems.

The bases of the *expectancy* of the existence of a God lie in the early patterns of childhood conditioning. During this period, when each of us is totally dependent on our parental figures, the association between helplessness and calling on God stimuli for assistance is established. The procedures by which this expectation is acquired are discussed in Chapter 6.

The longest section (Chapter 7) analyzes the role of language in the development of death anxiety. Language or some related symbolic system is the major means by which we anticipate our own demise long before it occurs. By using the appropriate combinations of God-related words, people from all human cultures have found ways to reduce the terror of this final termination.

All religious arguments are based on word games and appeal to simplistic, emotionally loaded concepts that pivot on deep feelings that are felt to be of special significance. The techniques by which religious behaviors are incorporated into the social fabric of a culture are discussed in Chapter 8. Although the rationale may change from religion to religion, the implementations are surprisingly similar.

The characteristics of the religious personality are reviewed in Chapter 9. Some people are prone to multiple experiences, whereas others display only one or two in a lifetime. Do people in the latter category fill the ranks of the habitual churchgoer? Are the former prone to more pathological displays when they are converted to a cause? The dangerous thinking of a religious personality faced with a complex political decision is also examined in detail.

The final chapter compares the intrinsic positive and negative potentials of the God Experience. If the God Experience is deeply rooted within the structure of the human brain, are there specific stimuli that will unleash it? We know that some social conditions evoke massive revival manias. Are there *natural* events that can trigger displays as well? If specific electrical patterns in the brain *are* the God Experience, could advanced technology be used to control human populations?

There are also positive possibilities. Some of the most unusual and promising discoveries of modern medicine include the curative effects of procedures that precipitate the God Experience. Are there certain aspects of human personality that are totally under the control of parental stimuli? Can they be generalized to a God belief and be used effectively to modify the diseases of the body?

This book is the synthesis of several years of clinical and academic investigation. Data from case histories were collected from interviews with normal people, before, during, and after periods of personal crisis. Most of the neuropsychological conclusions are based on experiments initially intended to elucidate the neural basis of paranormal experiences. It became evident, very quickly, that a more fundamental mental and pervasive phenomenon was being tested.

The systematic extrapolations from the concepts presented in this text were sometimes as surprising to myself as they will be to the reader. There is no attempt to embarrass any particular group of believers. My basic premise has been: If something is true, then no amount of challenge will ever change it.

Neuropsychological Bases of God Beliefs

1

Introduction: The Importance of Predicting the God Experience

The neuropsychological basis of God Beliefs is the primary theme of this text. God Beliefs are extraordinarily frequent and pervasive behaviors that are displayed in predictable situations. They have determined political strategies and precipitated national conflicts. They have inspired some generations and decimated others. However, the objective understanding of the psychological and neurobiological sources that determine the existence of God Beliefs has been conspicuously avoided. Considering their propensity to emerge during complex and insoluble, personal and public crises, the factors that control God Beliefs should be clearly delineated.

There are two basic components of God Beliefs: the God *Experience* and the God *Concept*. Although the specific details of each expression vary with personal experience and cultural conditioning, first-order characteristics are discriminable. God Experiences are transient phenomena that are loaded with emotional references. The nature of the experiences is influenced by the specific portion of the brain from which they originate. God Concepts are determined by verbal conditioning. They are derived from multiple references to stories about the origin of the culture. The concepts are maintained by the power of peer-group affinity, social pressure, and the individual's identification with the group.

The God Experience exists for a few seconds or minutes at any given time. Multiple experiences can occur in quick succession. During this period, the person feels that the "self," or some reference indicating "the thinking entity" becomes united with or "at one" with the symbolic form of all space-time. It may be called Allah, God, Cosmic Consciousness, or even some idiosyncratic label. Slightly deviant forms include references to intellectual abstracts such as "mathematical balance," "consciousness of time," or "extraterrestrial intrusions." These phenomena are similar to mystical states and the more secular "peak experiences."

Usually the God Experience involves euphoric and positive emotions. The person reports a type of God high that is characterized by a sense of profound meaningfulness, peacefulness, and cosmic serenity. Invariably the state is perfused with references to reduction of death anxiety. It is defined as the anticipated extinction of the self-concept or "the thinking entity." During the God Experience, the person suddenly feels that he or she will not die. Instead, he or she will live forever as a part or subset of the symbol of all space-time. If the symbol is a father image, then the person expects to become a child of the father. If the symbol is "imageless," the person expects to become a part of the Universal Whole.

Sometimes God Experiences can have negative emotional valences. During these periods, the same sense of oneness is pervaded by anxiety and fear. It is the epitome of terror. These experiences rarely happen more than once, except in psychiatric patients; the consequences punish any further display. Labels applied to these experiences reflect the bad, aversive or generally evil components of the culture in which the person survives. Classic references involve "hell," "demon world," or the more abstract "nether world." They are not traditionally called God Experiences, although they are certainly derived from the same source of variance. The self, with respect to space-time and imminent dissolution (death), still dominates the experience.

God Experiences occur once every few years within the normal person. When multiple events occur within a week, they are usually given special labels such as "revelations," "communions," or "conversions." Given minimal epileptic contributions, God Experiences are precipitated by personal crises, such as the loss of a loved one (real or imagined) or the confrontation of an insoluble problem. Certainly the greatest insoluble problem is the anticipation of self-extinction. Death anxiety increases in incremental steps as the person ages and approaches the latter portion of life. God Experiences proliferate during these periods and may even occur as death-bed episodes. The God Experience is followed by a remarkable anxiety reduction and a positive anticipation of the future.

God Concepts are dependent on verbal descriptors and conditioned language expectations of the culture. They invariably reflect the *reward patterns* of social behaviors. If the concept is paired with the label "father," then the expectations may be colored by images of an elderly bearded humanoid. The specific interactions with a reinforcing male may further determine the subtleties of the anticipation of the consistency in the delivery of rewards and punishments. Adult shifts in the self-concept, particularly due to education, also shape the conceptual format.

The God Concept and the verbal definitions of the self are highly interrelated. Simple associations such as "I am a Christian," "I am a Moslem," "I am a Buddhist," or even "I am an atheist" allow an intricate mixture of meanings between religious words and the self-concept. The God Concept is subject to powerful political manipulation. By indirect associations, such as "they have offended Allah" or "they have offended God," "they" are perceived as *personally* aversive. In this manner, large hoards of believers with shared God Concepts can be stimulated toward political ends.

The psychological potency of the God Concept, like the God Experience, is also coupled to the sense of death survival. Reduction of death anxiety or existential anxiety (the apprehension of living) is a fundamental derivative of the God Concept. The believer expects to survive death in some form, usually described as a variant of consciousness. Since the latter is viewed, inaccurately, by most people as not having any physical component, reference to a spiritual continuation is common. God Beliefs provide a reduction of the anxiety that would incapacitate most people and send others into an autistic stupor.

Since God Beliefs markedly attenuate death anxiety, they tend to proliferate within cultures that contain clear and imminent catastrophes. God Beliefs are also epidemic within cultures that have undergone change too quickly. The sudden shift in social patterns can be just as disconcerting and disruptive as daily disasters. Revitalization movements whose central theme is a return to the old and tried God Concepts can be simple solutions to the anxiety generated by novelty, uncertainty, and complexity.

Each person's God Belief is composed of a *combination* of the God Experience(s) and the God Concept. Some individuals may have very primitive or poorly socialized God Concepts; however, these people may have multiple God Experiences. Frequently these people are classified as mystics or eccentrics. Still other individuals may have never had a significant God Experience; but they may still have very powerful and strong God Concepts. Early and maintained relationships between the individual and the God Concept, such as weekly attendance at a church, mosque, synagogue, or religious area, maintain the God Belief.

The most rabid religious believer is the individual who has a strong God Concept and has had a God Experience that is compatible with the concept. These individuals are totally convinced of the validity of their experiences and the absolute truth of the God Concept. They may kill or sacrifice themselves for its benefit. But this generalization may not be explicit. It may only be inferred through the subtle entanglements of language association. They are frequently experienced as "compulsions" or "divine dictations."

Even the professed atheist displays some form of God Belief. If the behavior of atheists rather than their verbal displays are measured, then God Beliefs are evident. There are still references to the relationship between the self and the extensions of space and time. Death may be a final termination, but this known finality can be a source of anxiety reduction for people with certain types of reward history. More often, the atheist simply substitutes the conventional God Concept for abstract forms of mysticism. The "Great Nothingness" is almost indiscriminable from the Cosmic Whole of some Asian religions.

God Beliefs are highly correlated with *religious behaviors*. They include stereotyped response sequences, such as rituals with the hands or body and repeated phrases. Many body rituals include positions of primate submission, such as kneeling or prostrate displays. They are predictable from the part of the brain involved with the God Experience. Verbal sequences are designed to induce relaxation or general quiescence, and are substitutes for the poetry and prose of more secular surroundings. The phrases are primarily associated with the God Concept and contain taboos for derogatory or humorous exploitation.

Religious behaviors are correlated with God Beliefs but may not be determined by them. Religious behaviors within a group may be maintained by a variety of nonbelief factors such as peer-group comradery or the inference of social or economic rewards (the businessman approach), or simply by the prevalence of the religious behaviors throughout the person's reward history. In a world where everything changes, the church, synagogue, or mosque becomes the only source of stability and consistency.

To understand these important human behaviors, a theory has been carefully developed. Three essential processes are postulated. First, the potential to display God Experiences is due to particular evolutionary developments within the human brain. Second, the anticipation of the God Concept is derived from the pattern of early relationships between infant and parents. Third, organized religious behaviors are generated by the intrinsic properties of human language, including thought. All three processes are organized by their consequences through the mechanisms of learning.

Do not misunderstand the theme of this text. There *are* many positive aspects of religious behaviors. They can foster hope and stimulate creativity. Faith in gods can give structure in the midst of chaos and make the world a psychologically safe place in which to live. Religious behaviors can reduce the anxiety of the unknown and tame the terror of global unpredictability.

Unfortunately, there are several negative features of God Experiences. They nurture a resistant strain of egoism. Although it is masked by a pleasant smile, religions encourage the conclusion that the believer is somehow special and unique. The believers of the Koran feel that it is just a little more valid than the Bible, and the believers of the Bible feel it is just a little more valid than the Koran.

Each believer feels that his or her experience is more true and more real than those of others. Friendly lip-service is given to liberal understanding. Sometimes maverick peacemakers attempt to show that all religions are different experiences of the same thing. But deep down, the feelings of uniqueness remain.

It is a common, normal feeling that pervades all of us. The feeling that "I am somehow special" is the driving force behind the success of far-fetched possibilities such as lotteries. Each person feels that he or she will be favored in some special way. It is a persistent illusion that is encouraged by religious organizations.

Because of the unusual but predictable learning history of human beings, personal experience is also used as proof. A person believes in the existence of questionable phenomena because "I have seen them" or rejects their occurrence because "I have not seen them." Even the skeptic who contends that God does not exist will say, "There is no deity, but you know, when *my* father died, I heard the voice. . . . "

The egocentric reference of proof is reinforced by the intense, complicated emotions paired with the development of the self-concept. When these feelings occur, facts and formulae and years of objectivity may be forgotten in a single moment. It's like the statement of a recent author before his death: "I always knew death happens to everyone—the history of the world shows that, only I thought in my case an exception would be made."

When such egoism becomes the property of groups, it becomes dangerous. When people of similar beliefs cluster together, the idea of mutual understanding soon fades into the problem of superior and inferior. Other people are no longer different; instead, they are inferior, unenlightened, or just plain stupid.

The consequences of such thinking have destroyed more people in the name of God than natural catastrophes. Think of the missionaries of the previous four centuries who systematically destroyed each non-Western culture because its people did not believe as they did. Complex and sophisticated societies of Africa, the Americas, and the Pacific Ocean were razed in the name of profit and religious zeal.

Of course, there were the opportunists—the political manipulators, the militarists, the emerging capitalists—who took advantage of the spoils. However, these atrocities were not perpetrated by people who were deviant or insane; they were just more conspicuous. These devastations were committed by *average* people who shared the belief that they had the *only* answer.

This dark side of egoism starts as a subtle thing. Well-intentioned people begin with a desire to share the gifts of their insights with others. When others do not share the enthusiasm, rationales emerge, like "we must save them for their own good because they are so ignorant, but they will be thankful later." It starts with simple group exclusion and ends with execution.

Death and denial are crude forms of the exclusion produced by the egoism of the group. There is also a more subtle form—the exclusion of ideas. The belief that "my ideas are the only right ideas" soon leads to the dictation of what can be said and thought. If enough people believe the same thing, the restriction of ideas can become law.

When thinking is constricted and rabid opinion becomes enforced by who is strongest, alternative possibilities are not pursued. It is assumed that certain ideas are dangerous or not fit for consumption. Books are placed on prohibited lists and forms of potentially productive research are denied.

This is the most dangerous form of group exclusion. Whereas death and denial of other people have clear and immediate consequences, the smothering of ideas is less clear. Only later does the impact from this uneven thwarting of human potential become evident.

Religious mentality and an egocentric addiction to the God Experience also rely on proofs based on hearsay. Although these proofs may be punctuated by the person's individual experience, a dependence is developed on what *others* have said or written about their beliefs. There are no references to independent checks or numerical measurements or the objective testing of counter-arguments. Instead, the person believes because "someone told me so."

The reliance on other people's beliefs, especially if they are older (or lived a thousand years ago), is another negative component of religious experiences. Once again, it is an extreme form of a normal human behavior whose presence is so pervasive that it is ignored. But you can hear it when the child asks, "Why can't I go to town?" and the parent answers, "Because I told you so." Or, "Why is the sky blue?" "Because I told you so." Most of us do not grow up in an environment of data or reason but in an atmosphere of "someone told you so."

While we are children, we abhor this form of adult superiority. No amount of rationality or reason appears to dissuade the parent from his or her egocentric course. We tell ourselves we will never be like that with our children. Then one day we catch ourselves, usually in a moment of frustration or irritability, saying, "The world cannot be changed because I said so."

In a more powerful and pervasive way, this form of proof by authority is found within the ranks of every religious organization. People who believe in the Bible argue its proof by saying "because it says so in the Bible." People who believe in the Tibetan Book of the Dead say the same about their scripture.

This reliance on nonexplanation is a major deterrent to the pursuit of new ideas; it eliminates the enthusiasm of the open mind and dampens the determination required for discovery. With this mentality, there is no option to test ideas or to pursue new concepts. Numbers are dismissed for jargon phrases such as, "If it was good enough for my father, it's good enough for me." Objectivity is replaced by the arbitrary decision of personal experience. The search for knowledge is killed, coldly and without deliberation, because "it is written" somewhere.

From this basic assumption is generated perhaps the most ridiculous cliché ever stated, that there are just some things people should not investigate. With this mentality, certain questions about human origins cannot be asked; specific assumptions cannot be made. An entire dimension of human potential becomes a forbidden zone.

Religious beliefs have an odd property. Charged by the conviction of egocentricity, each person believes her or his assumptions about where she or he came from and where she or he is going. People spend lifetimes extending the logic of their God Experiences with the care and precision of the most cautious scientist. Their entire lives become endless trials of verification and personal testimony.

But at the same time, *they never challenge the basic assumptions of the beliefs*. Despite their arguments and sophisticated statements, they assume that the information is true merely because it's written on some old pages, because it has been believed for centuries, because "someone told them so," because they believe they have experienced it.

Not surprisingly, these people have a contempt for the science of psychology. The analysis of human behavior is misinterpreted, ignored, or dismissed as so much drivel. Since the basic assumptions of behavioral science emphasize the objective evaluation of human experience, it challenges the arbitrary nature of beliefs.

The slightest likelihood that personal experience is *not* a valid measure of anything is a frightening feature for the believer. His or her entire system of proofs about God and the self are threatened. By trivializing the significance of behavioral analyses, the threat is removed and personal confidence is restored.

Religious behaviors shaped around God Experiences foster an unhealthy dependence on the belief that "someone" out there will rescue the world from its problems. It encourages the submission to assumptions of superior beings, who, in the moment of humanity's greatest desperations, will intervene and save its soul. This dependence is the final negative component of the God Experience.

God Beliefs maintain a form of *conditioned helplessness* whereby assumptions are made that certain problems are beyond human solution. They reinforce a schizoid condition in which people use their intelligence to solve technical problems, but, at the same time, kneel in submission to God, who conducts human affairs.

This helplessness distorts and interferes with the human potential. Unproven assumptions are made that humanity cannot guide itself or that it must obtain guidance from some superior being in order to survive. Unsubstantiable contentions are kept alive. Only gods or some surrogate of extraterrestrial intelligence must have the answer.

There is an epidemic of such contradictory behavior. On one hand, we train our children to use their brains to crack the concepts of nature. We solve the complex problems of the atom and unravel the genetic potential of the DNA helix. We derive the solutions of relativistic equations and determine answers to great technical questions of our time. We do this by systematic extrapolation and the unending challenge to basic assumptions.

But at the same time, we train our children, either directly or by our actions, to fall on their knees to solve personal difficulties. People are taught that ultimate solutions for personal destiny and the future of the human race rest with superior beings whose nature and power can be suspected but never demonstrated.

The conditional helplessness generated by extreme religious beliefs destroys our versatility. We begin to believe that people cannot possibly solve their personal problems. We begin to expect that certain things are beyond our grasp. So we relinquish our potential, throw away proven methods, close our eyes, and walk blindly within the shadows of religious experience.

There is great danger in this conceptual contradiction. As long as there are no crises and daily life runs smoothly, conditioned helplessness is not evident. People solve their business affairs by the principles of human behavior. Scientists determine detailed solutions by the sweat of human trial and error. Housewives solve their complexities with the potential of the human brain.

However, when there is a crisis, the consequences of helplessness beome evident. While the world collapses, people do not think or solve or challenge with alternatives. Instead, they pray or kneel or scream for cosmic intervention, like panicked people in a room on fire. The solution is to stop, to think, and to *open* the door.

It is so easy, when problems appear beyond solution, to turn away and wait for outside help. It is attractive when times are tough to ignore the hard work of problem solving and to regress to simple ideas from a thousand years ago. The past is safe; it has already happened. There is no anxiety there.

But we can't live in the past. We live in a complex world full of indefinite possibilities. Human behavior cannot be reduced to a few naive categories of good and bad or body and spirit. Such words may be charged with emotional associations, but they do not change poverty or predict national confrontations.

There is a great need to understand the biological and behavioral basis of God Concepts and the God Experience. The potential long-term negative effects of these behaviors on human survival must be considered now. If God Beliefs are true, then there is no difficulty.

However, suppose they are not totally correct? In the last four hundred years, some of humanity's most cherished beliefs have been destroyed. It is no longer the center of the universe, or a unique creation of the animal kingdom, or a totally rational presence. Gradually, despite the protests, some of humanity's egocentric beliefs have been removed. One of the remaining and most profound infrastructures of the human psyche is the God Experience.

2
The Temporal Lobe: The Biological Basis of the God Experience

The extraordinary development of the human brain cannot be denied. Whether this change is considered to be a product of long evolution or of sudden occurrence does not alter the profound importance of the development. With the increased size of the brain relative to body mass, the human species obtained an unprecedented ability to comprehend the universe.

Certainly the most important change for the later emergence of human societies was the enlargement of the frontal lobes (see Figure 1). This portion of the human brain occupies about one-half of the total cerebral capacity. Its proliferation allowed the predominance of two important behaviors: the ability to inhibit and the ability to anticipate.

The ability to inhibit impulses was primary to the survival of even the first social groups. Groups cannot be maintained unless the impulses of the component individuals are kept in check. When each member feeds or fights or copulates according to selfish and egocentric impulses, the group behavior deteriorates. The culture dies.

Modern society is replete with inhibitions. They are translated as "Thou shalt not." We cannot kill a person because we feel like it; we cannot engage in sex with another whenever it suits us. We must learn to inhibit our behaviors. As long as the human brain can inhibit, complex societies can be maintained.

People who have not learned to inhibit, either because of inadequate training or due to some biological error, are considered the criminals of a culture. They are removed from its presence and killed or preserved in some safe place. Such people cannot be allowed to run free if the society is to survive.

The ability to inhibit contributes to clear logic and sharp thinking. During problem solving, we can exclude or inhibit the thousands of memories or thoughts

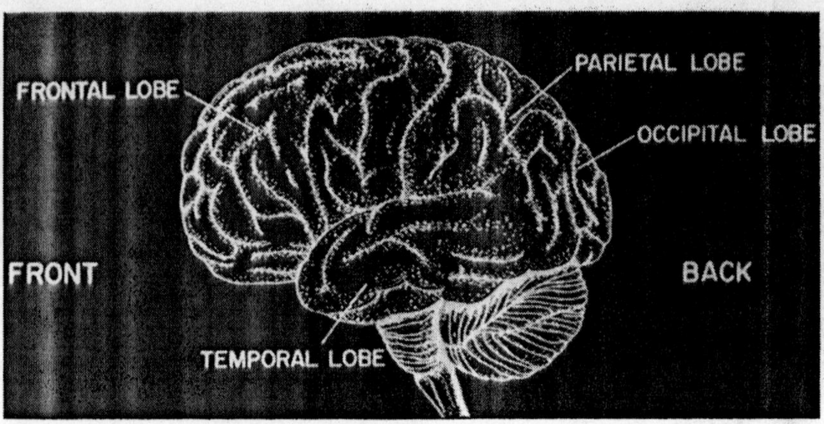

Figure 1. A drawing of the human brain from a side perspective. The major lobes are indicated.

that could interfere. Instead, we can concentrate upon a crossword puzzle, talk about politics to a buddy in a bar, or calculate the size of distant galaxies.

People who cannot inhibit irrelevant responses do not talk or think in clear and crisp patterns. These people free associate, talk in nonsense, and confuse words and phrases. Sometimes they are called schizophrenics; most of the time they are just called crazy. For a variety of different medical reasons, they have a chronic lack of ability to inhibit.

The ability to inhibit is a fragile commodity within each of us. Its strength is weakened by alcohol, fatigue, and mind-bending drugs. During these periods of intoxication, concentration is difficult and memory comes and goes. Images of hate, impulses of revenge and sexual desires, typically inhibited by a history of punishment, emerge into awareness.

The second consequence of the frontal lobes is the capacity to anticipate. As the frontal lobe grew larger and more complex, the human species began to anticipate not just the next few seconds or days, but an entire life. Accompanying this anticipation was the experience of time.

Prediction and anticipation have great survival value for the human species. They are the foundation for hopes and idealistic goals. They allow the development of complex technologies and sophisticated social systems.

However, anticipation is a two-edged sword. As long as the anticipated event is positive in nature, great strides are made. People work to save for the future. Children are conceived to replenish the race and crops are planted for the expected harvest. These anticipations are associated with the joy and vicarious identification of endless survival.

What the human species gained in the ability to plan and to anticipate, it paid for by the experience of anxiety and apprehension. When the anticipated event is negative, we do not experience happiness or an expectation of fulfillment. Instead, we are debilitated by feelings of doom.

During such a period, we are incapacitated. The ability to think is lost and all the fine discriminations fade into one confusing, confining form. We feel our hearts pump, and the walls of the room appear to move in around us. Sometimes we feel like we are about to die.

And that's the crux of the problem. With the ability to anticipate the future, the human brain also developed the potential to acknowledge self-death. We can plan and make great structures, but we can also anticipate our own demise.

Death is the end of individual experience, the time when the thing you call your "self" appears to terminate. It is perhaps the greatest unknown of them all. By its very definition, it contains the terrors of our most horrific human imaginations. The consequences can be devastating.

However, at the same time the frontal lobes were burgeoning with their capacity to inhibit and to anticipate, another part of the human brain was changing. This portion of the brain, called the temporal lobe, also grew in size and expanded outward from the sides of the major mass (Fig. 2).

The structure of the temporal lobe was aptly formed for the demands of the new human brain. It contained a central area where sounds could be experienced and understood either in space or in time. Through connections to the frontal lobe and other portions of the brain, regions of the temporal lobe contributed to speech.

This sudden development of the capacity to speak was highly correlated with the ability to think. By processes that are not yet technically clear, these properties were preconditions for the appearance of the phenomena known as awareness and experience.

The developments did not end here. Two important structures, the *hippocampus* and the *amygdala*, began to migrate deep within the brain (Fig. 3). As the neocortex grew in size, the hippocampus was slowly pushed backward and down to the side of the brain until it rested in the temporal lobe. The amygdala was pushed, laterally, away from its origin in the smell brain, to within the lobe as well.

The appearance of these two structures within the temporal lobe contributed to two important properties: the experience of *remembering* and *evaluation*. With the development of these structures, experiences could be labelled as rewarding or punishing. More importantly, they could be remembered.

To accommodate this expansion, marked variations in the brain's architecture occurred. An extra fold or convolution appeared within the primate cortex immediately adjacent to the hippocampus. From this new region emerged massive fibers that sent out and received information from all over the brain.

The hippocampus became a gateway to the experience of images (Issacson and Pribram 1975). Appropriate stimulation of this region of the human brain could unleash a vivid stream of past memories. It could also initiate an inundation of rich fantasy over which the experiencer had little control. One of

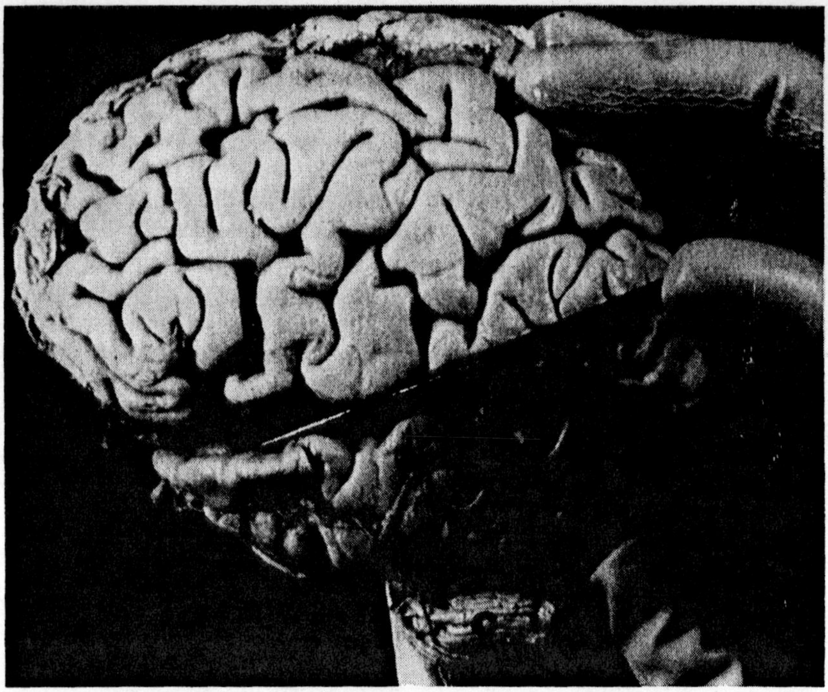

Figure 2. Photograph of a human brain from a side perspective (same perspective as in Figure 1). Below the probe (which is inserted into the Sylvian fissure or lateral sulcus) is the region of the temporal lobe. Below it is the cerebellum (c).

these processes, whose intimacy with memory consolidation is clearly evident, was the experience of dreams.

The amygdala became a control center for the display and experience of emotions and moods (Plutchik and Kellerman 1986). The potential for fight or flight and the experience of anger or fear evolved together (Eleftheriou 1972). With the coupling of these emotions to mood, the human animal could experience the heights of euphoria and the depths of depression.

Because of connections to the frontal lobes and upper portions of the temporal lobe, these emotions became mixed with the experiences of the self. The sensations of being a person, a real entity, a unique thing in this universe, became tied to the guts of the organism. With this mixing came the exhilaration of self-preservation and the fear of personal extinction.

A biological capacity for the God Experience was critical for the survival of the species. Without some experiences that could balance the terror of personal extinction, existence of the human phenomenon called the "self" could not be

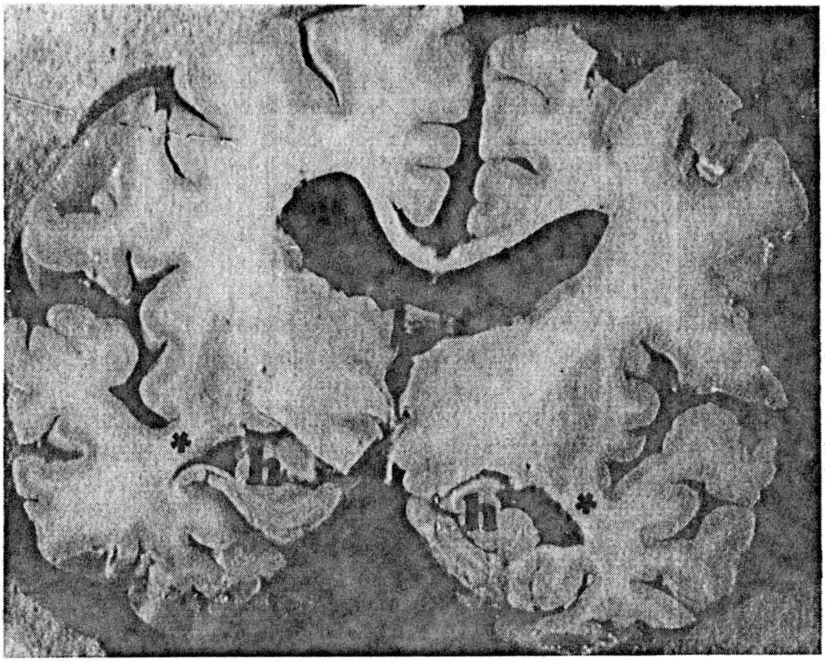

Figure 3. A coronal section of the human brain. The two large "holes" in the middle of the section are the lateral ventricles. The temporal lobes include the major section on the lower, lateral portions of the brain (the lobes are attached effectively to the rest of the brain at this section by the tissue indicated by the asterisks). The hippocampal areas (indicated by h) are located deep within the temporal lobes. Along this same plane, in a back-to-front direction, lies the amygdala.

maintained. It would have been fragmented by the persistent, gnawing realization that death could come at any time.

Initially, the God Experience may not have had a particular representation. Although there is no known way to re-create the experiences of the first human brain as it contemplated this cosmic event, the first experience may have been a kind of "cosmic serenity."

It was probably much like the Hindu–Buddhist concept of Nirvana (Murphy and Murphy 1968), whereby the person experiences a quiescence. Within this quiescence, there is no fear, no anxiety, only the sensation of becoming a part of everything. The words may be poetry but the survival value is real—the person can cope with anticipation of self-annihilation.

The capacity to have the God Experience is a consequence of the human brain's construction. If the temporal lobe had developed in some other way, the God Experience would not have occurred. I am not contending that the experience of God is localized within the temporal lobe, no more than vision is stored within the occipital lobe or the body image is stored within the parietal region. Instead, my hypothesis is that the God Experience is a phenomenon that is associated with the construction of the temporal lobe.

All of us, by virtue of our primate heritage, have this capacity. Some of us may regress to it, others may enhance it, and still others may be embarrassed by its presence. Like the propensity to walk and to talk, it is a potential in each of us. We may just know it by different names.

Of course, the best test of this idea would be to compare our species with a similar form that did not have the same development of the temporal lobe. Optimally, this fictional creature would have the same development of the other portions of the brain but without the odd positioning of the hippocampus and amygdala or the massive connections between the temporal and frontal lobes. To date, such a comparison has not been possible.

Instead, to test the neurobiological basis of the God Experience, we must look at people who have minute alterations in this region. If all human beings have the innate capacity to have a God Experience, then those individuals with appropriate alterations in the temporal lobe should report enhanced occurrences. Although the details should be highly variable, they would show the general themes of religious behavior.

Such changes can be determined within the temporal lobe. The hippocampus, for example, is notoriously prone to deterioration due to insufficient blood supply, inadequate oxygen levels, or deficits in essential nutrients. Because of the odd geometry of its blood vessels, the hippocampus is prone to deterioration from thickening of the arteries.

Even a small deterioration in temporal lobe tissue produces pronounced and crude behaviors. Damage to the hippocampus produces some of the densest amnesias known to medical science. However, when there is no memory there is no past, and when there is no past there is little anticipation of a future.

The test cannot be carried out on the behaviors of severely damaged brains. People with severe brain damage have exaggerated experiences where fragments of normal behaviors are amplified to bizarre extremes. To conclude that God Experiences are a consequence of brain damage would contradict their functional significance, unless one assumes that brain damage has survival value.

Instead, a more subtle and reversible alteration in the temporal lobe's activity must be chosen. Aberrant electrical activity deep within the temporal lobe is one such candidate. God Experiences do not occur all the time, at least in most of us. They occur in short bursts during periods of personal crisis, following ingestions of chemicals, or after certain rituals (such as prayer) have been followed.

Although electrical changes reflect alterations in the functional structure of the brain, they may not always be permanent. Some electrical changes reflect the intrinsic cluster properties of the millions of neurons involved. The *degree* to which these neurons are likely to maintain any electrical instability, however, is related to their location and to the alteration of appropriate neuronal chemicals. They are called *transmitters* and form the effective communication between the brain cells.

When electrical criteria are considered, the temporal lobe maintains a unique position among neural tissues. Hippocampal cells, in particular, display more electrical instability than any other portion of the brain. These cells are also prone to repeated firing long after the stimulation has been removed (Haracz 1984).

The usefulness of this sensitivity can be seen in its function. Since the hippocampus is so important for the consolidation of experience (what we call memory), a sensitivity to the variety of complex and subtle inputs to the eyes, ears, and visceral senses is critical. As we search our complex environment, it must be given not only structure but meaning.

Electrical lability leads to unique properties. The amygdala and the hippocampus can *learn* specific electrical patterns. Like the total person learning to drive a car or to play tennis, specific kinds of electrical activity can be slowly acquired by these structures. This means that the experiences associated with those electrical patterns can come under the control of a place (like a church), a time (like crisis), or even more ominous, a person.

Learned electrical changes within the brain are integrated within the intrinsic patterns of activity. Different regions of the brain show particular patterns that more or less reflect structure and function. The temporal lobe is no exception. One of the most frequent electrical patterns generated from this lobe is called *theta activity*.

Theta activity, which has been defined as slow, synchronous or slightly spiked waves with frequencies between 4 and 7 hertz (cycles/second) is associated with alterations in temporal lobe function. These waves occur during dreaming, creative thinking, and twilight states. This activity is present when you hear your name called just before you fall asleep. It is active when you close your eyes and repeat some thought, prayer, or mantra until only a pleasant floating sensation remains.

Most of the time, the electrical activity of the temporal lobe is not exceptional. During thinking and experiencing, the billions of neurons within the region maintain a complex field of electromagnetic patterns. There are few experiences of god, few episodes of intense meaning, and little sense of cosmic serenity.

But, as we know, there are brief periods, such as those occurring late at night, when the threshold of the God Experiences can be approached. Sometimes, in the early morning hours as we concentrate on some meaningful task, the sense of solitude blends into an odd feeling of familiarity. We begin to experience thoughts as if they have occurred before. A presence is sensed but not seen.

There are times when the complexities of the world bear too much upon us. The job, the family and the six o'clock news wear away our thin veneer of invulnerability. Just as life appears worthless and futile, we suddenly experience a sense of understanding and a feeling of knowing. The next morning we can move again, forgetting, sometimes with shame, the convictions of the night before.

There are periods in each of our lives when we begin to know our dreams will never be acknowledged. As we pass from the third into the fourth decade of life, the youthful exuberation of infinite possibilities fragments into a cold reality of the mediocre. And then we hear a voice call us and we call it God. The next day, renewed and refreshed, we begin again.

These experiences should be correlated with normal, transient electrical perturbations of the human temporal lobe. For now, they will be called *temporal lobe transients* (Persinger 1983). When they occur, the innate feelings of the God Experience are displayed. Depending on the extent of the activity, some experiences would be mild cosmic highs, the kind we feel in the early morning hours when a hidden truth becomes sudden knowledge. Other more intense transients would evoke the peak experiences of life and determine it thereafter. They would involve religious conversions, rededications, and personal communions with God.

The first time I recorded an inconspicuous electrical seizure from the temporal lobe of a meditator and heard the reports of cosmic bliss, I was impressed with the impact of this change on the person's behavior (Persinger, 1984a). Here sat a person waiting with anticipation for the coming of a few short seconds of seizure. There were no convulsions or head movements of any kind, just a slight smile and the facial expressions of cosmic serenity.

But the experience was compelling. The individual, depressed and forlorn before the episode, left with a fresh view of the world. For a few brief seconds, the person had mingled with the Great Mentality whose rudiments are found in every human culture. The person had experienced a conviction shared by millions of other individuals.

These people are not "weirdos" or diagnosed abnormals. They are average people who interact in everyday ways with other people. They cope with their jobs, talk to their children, and carry on complex conversations. Some of them are the leaders of the scientific and artistic worlds.

I never had the heart to tell that first person about the electrical recordings. In fact, the realization that the God Experience could be an artifact of the human brain was intellectually paralyzing. But since then, like hundreds of other brain scientists (Dewhurst and Beard 1970; Hermann and Whitman 1984) who have been determined to separate semantics from science, I have observed the symptoms again and again.

They can be seen at the peak of prayer, when people revel in spiritual transcendence. They can be seen during revivals when the sound of emotional hymns bring tears and smiles and the sense of a lifted burden. Wherever the world falls apart or loved ones die, the patterns appear.

The power of the God Experience shames any known therapy. With a single burst in the temporal lobe, people find structure and meaning in seconds. With it comes the personal conviction of truth and the sense of self-selection. How many people have died, still smiling, on arena floors and battlefields, in anticipation of another single burst of activity?

The last question does not stem from cynicism but from concern. If the God Experience can control the lives of human beings to this extreme, what if it can be controlled or manipulated by things or people? If the God Experience is a biological artifact of the human brain, no amount of consoling words from ancient scriptures will alter that potential. The only difference between old works and modern books is the age of the paper.

That temporal lobe transients exist within us all has not been proven (yet); however, it can be inferred. If temporal lobe transients are like any other phenomena, they should be distributed along a statistical continuum. Most of us should have small ones once or twice a year, while a few of us should have them more frequently. A small percentage should show intense and extreme bouts of temporal lobe transients, and by virtue of the brain's construction, display convulsions. Such a population exists; they have been called *temporal lobe epileptics* (Bear and Fedio 1977).

There is nothing unusual about studying the exception in order to find the rule. By studying people with problems in the frontal lobes, neuroscientists determined the correlates of thinking, abstracting, and planning for the future. By studying people with peculiar parietal regions, researchers revealed how the awareness of the body image is learned. We have gleaned a great deal about this great raveled knot by noting its occasional deviations.

Temporal lobe epilepsy is a special form of epileptic disorder. Unlike the more publicized types of petit mal (when the person blacks out for a brief period) or grand mal seizure (when the person has a "fit"), temporal lobe epilepsy is not necessarily associated with convulsions.

To state that temporal lobe epilepsy is a disease with distinct symptoms, like measles or even influenza, would be inappropriate. Since the primary reason for the diagnosis is unusual electrical activity in the (usually anterior) temporal lobe, there is much overinclusion. The different potential abnormalities within this volume of brain space produce a multitude of interactions.

However, the most persistent characteristic of the temporal lobe is the "psychic seizures" *without* accompanying convulsions. *Psychic seizure*, which is a relatively poor diagnostic label (and should not be confused with psychic research) refers to the experiences associated with abnormal electrical activity within the temporal lobe. People with seizures in this part of the brain experience vivid landscapes or perceive forms of living things. Some of these entities are not human, but are described as little men, glowing forms, or bright, shining sources.

The modality of the experience, that is, whether it is experienced as a sound, a smell, a scene (vision), or an intense feeling, reflects the area of the electrical instability. If the focus of the electrical activity is near a portion of the temporal lobe (like the uncus) associated with smell, then the experience may be olfactory. If the area of abnormal activity is near the auditory projection area, then the experience may involve sounds or voices.

The experiences, whether visual or auditory, may have actually happened or they may be mixtures of fantasy and reality. Sometimes they may be fixed in space and time, while in other cases they may be as dynamic as everyday experiences. However, whether they are dreamlike or as vivid as this book in front of you, they are experienced as real.

There are a number of changes that occur during psychic seizures that reflect the functions of the temporal lobe. The person may experience a sense of altered meaning. Sometimes there may be an enhanced sense of familiarity (déjà vu) with events that have never been experienced. At other times, the opposite, an enhanced sense of strangeness to well-known conditions, may occur.

The sense of meaningfulness is like conviction. During a psychic seizure, intense and profound feelings may occur. Afterwards the person may not remember the details, but be convinced that it happened. The event, although vague, is packed with personal and profound significance.

Another characteristic of this abnormality is an alteration in the description of the self. Depersonalization is typical. In this state, the person feels unreal or simply "not there." The body may appear to be in one place while the mind is in another. Depending on the person's learning, these experiences range from the heavenly to the exotic.

Frequently coupled to these symptoms is the experience of forced thinking. As the appropriate region of the temporal lobe displays abnormal electrical activity, repeated thoughts are experienced. They may be a phrase or a slogan or just a nonsense sequence. Again and again, they occur in a fixed stereotyped manner.

Perceptual alterations are usually limited to the sudden expansion of visual and auditory images. Objects in the room may suddenly seem to grow very small and then increase in size again. Sounds may fluctuate from very faint and distant to very loud and near.

Patients with temporal epilepsy or complex partial seizures are known to experience terror and incapacitating anxiety. Yet other times, they feel euphoric and happy with the enthusiastic sensation of unlimited possibilities. Irritability can lead to homicidal impulses, while depression precedes suicidal contemplations. These symptoms may not be associated with any kind of convulsion.

The coupling between temporal lobe disorders and religious experiences can be traced into antiquity (Dewhurst and Beard 1970). Shorn of their poetic language, the descriptions of most religious leaders indicate temporal lobe abnormalities. If they were alive today, they would have much less appeal. There appears to be something magical about psychiatric symptoms when they are centuries old (Trawick 1963).

When we resist our reflex tendency to accept the received gospel merely because it is written, the Joan of Arcs of our past are cast in another light.

There now appears to be good reason why they heard voices and then felt weak and incapacitated. There are clear mechanisms that explain why their sexual impulses waned when the euphoria of a cosmic high appeared. There is an explanation for seeing visions of things to come that never really came.

Now I am not saying that the experiences of God are synonymous with temporal lobe epilepsy. The experiences of the temporal lobe epileptic are exaggerated and disorganized forms of the brain's activity. When vast depolarizing waves spread across millions of cells, all types of memories and fantasies are mixed and mashed together. If the spreading is severe enough, even convulsions or "fits" may occur.

Instead, *the God Experience is a normal and more organized pattern of temporal lobe activity.* These short temporal lobe transients are precipitated by subtle psychological factors such as personal stress, loss of a loved one, and the dilemma of anticipated death. There are no convulsions and few bizarre behaviors.

When these small changes occur, they are experienced in an organized and balanced fashion. The experiences are primarily pleasurable and sublime characteristics of less severe forms of electrical activity. Only in more extreme conditions do fear and a sense of cosmic helplessness emerge.

But the potential is not all-or-none. By virtue of brain function, there is a continuum along which all of us will fall. Everyone of the more than four billion brains that compose the human species would be distributed along this scale. Most of us, by definition, fall in the middle.

The temporal lobe epileptic merely falls at one end of this continuum. They display the types of behaviors experienced by all of us, except they are more fragmented. Most of the time, the components—the fear or the sublime, the cosmic communion or the eternal helplessness—are distorted out of proportion or hidden within the confusion of the seizure.

However, the essential symptoms are seen in a milder manner within every type of religious experience that has been reported. The sense of profound knowing (Browning 1968) is experienced as "being touched by God" or "being at one with the universe." The depersonalization is reported as "soul travelling" or "an insight into the streets of heaven." Forced thinking is experienced as being "implanted with the words of God." A simple epileptic aura is experienced as the distant sound of heavenly choirs.

These patterns are clearer within the behaviors of temporal lobe patients between apparent seizures. During these periods, the brains of these people are most similar to the brains of average people during the peaks of frustration, stress, and personal crisis. It is during these times that the religious themes of thought and God Experiences should be and are evident.

In fact, the behavior of the temporal lobe epileptic has been characterized by the persistent theme of religiosity. Their lives are full of repeated peaks of mystical experiences and multiple conversions. They are obsessed by moral issues and the experiences of God and fulfillment (Geschwind 1983).

Not surprisingly, their behaviors and psychological experiences are predominated by a sense of personal destiny, the most supreme form of infantile egoism. Each one has been selected to give a message to the world. Like the committed preacher or the proselytizing prophet, they have a sense of the special—their experiences are somehow exceptional.

Whether prone to the ups of mania or the deep downs of depression, they are characterized by philosophical themes. Where did they come from? How were they born? Will they be reborn? Will they live forever? Sometimes the theme may be blatantly atheistic, but again and again they talk about the God Experience.

Indeed, there is something about the temporal lobe and religious experience that cannot be refuted. There's the experience of time and the implication of eternity. There's the experience of space and the implication of infinity. There's the feeling of the intense meaning of the beginning and the end of it all.

If the data are so clear, why haven't the patterns been evident? The relationship has been obscured by the source itself, the temporal lobe epileptic. First, most individuals who are hospitalized and systematically observed have other complications. The experiences they report are related to the nature of the more progressive disease processes (Slater and Beard 1963).

Second, when God Experiences do occur, they are not reported. Personal God Experiences, because of the profound implication for the person's destiny, are not mentioned, lest they be misconstrued. People have been taught to assume that images of their late Uncle Henry in a rocking chair, smoking a cigar, are hallucinations; but the experiences of God are real.

There is a way around the secrecy. Inhibition of ideas and actions are less evident within psychotic populations. Psychotic people, who are frequently called "just crazy," fail to inhibit their impulses. They cannot relate in a predictable fashion to the world around them, nor can they cope in any socially acceptable manner with the confusion and complexity of the change.

If temporal lobe disorders were associated with religiosity and the God Experience, then the temporal lobe *psychotic* should be a population inundated with these experiences. The data indicate this obsession. As reported by Slater and Beard (1963):

> Mystical delusional experiences are remarkedly common. One patient said that God, or an electrical power was making him do things; that he was the Son of God. Another said he felt God working a miracle on him. Another felt that God and the Devil were fighting within him and that God was winning. Another claimed, "All this goes into one vast electronic brain which gives God the power to give you life and individuality. . . . "
>
> Hallucinations were often extremely complex and were usually full of meaning, often of a mystical type. Nearly always there were auditory hallucinations at the same time. One patient saw God, heard voices and music and received a message that he was going

to heaven. Another had a vision of Christ on the cross in the sky, and heard the voice of God saying, "You will be healed, your tears have been seen."

Indeed, these reports are from hospitalized people. But does that change the impact of their experiences? Psychotic individuals are *not* psychological lepers or inhuman creatures. Their difference from normal people is only one of degree (and this is arbitrary). The same behaviors they display every day, we display once or twice in 20 years.

Most of us have learned to compartmentalize the God Experience. It can be conditioned to occur in specific places or during certain times. Because of the relationship between the frontal and the temporal lobes, most of us can learn to inhibit—to control—its occurrence. Only in the psychotic does it run rampant.

Certainly, I am not the first neuroscientist to suggest the connection. Many others have seen it before. Most have denied it. A few, frightened by the implications, have pushed it into the corners of institutions. There it stayed, pigeonholed, as an abnormal mental event that is never outwardly manifested. I also suspect that some practitioners even guard it, as if its escape would bring global havoc. Neuroscientists are, after all, human beings with fears of personal extinction and desires for immortality.

3
Predicting Brain Factors in the God Experience

If the potential for the God Experience is due to the basic structure of the temporal lobe of the human brain, then any series of conditions that lead to the occurrence of temporal lobe transients (TLTs) should also be associated with the experience. By knowing the normal behaviors correlated with the temporal lobe, not only the basic characteristics but the places and times of the God Experience can be predicted.

The general features of the God Experience, although colored by the language of different cultures, are basically the same. A first cluster of symptoms is the profound meaningful nature of the experience (no matter how mundane the situation) and a sense of understanding between the self and the cosmos. In the latter case, the cosmos may be experienced in more concrete terms, such as a parent substitute—a male or female spirit, depending on the culture.

Like the psychic seizure of temporal lobe epileptics, the God Experience may not involve clear details. The person is convinced that the experience occurred, yet he or she cannot recall the specifics. All he or she remembers is that *something* important, profound, and deeply religious (or mystical) took place.

The gut feeling of the experience is an extension of the sense of familiarity and the alteration in evaluative capacity of the epileptic seizure. For a brief moment, during the temporal lobe transients, the person peers into another realm and experiences familiarity. This other realm has many names: heaven, the world of spirits, or the other dimensions.

Christian conversions, especially those associated with great emotional commitment (as opposed to simple peer-group pressure) frequently display this characteristic. For example, one individual who had had a religious experience in his early adulthood remembers:

At the time I was under great emotional duress, I didn't know what to do with my life. I spent my days drunk and my nights with loose women. Then suddenly, I felt the presence of God and just knew it was He. He called my name and I had the most joyous experience of my life, a Communion with the Creator.

When pressed for further details about the episode, this individual, like many other people who have had the God Experience, did not respond. People usually give a variety of excuses, such as, "It is a very personal thing and I don't wish to discuss it" or "This was a marvelous experience and should not be dissected in the light of modern analysis," or more simply, "None of your business." Typically, the statement is punctuated with the kind of smile that those who study religious experiences see time after time.

These individuals are not lying, nor are they purposely refusing comment. Like some epileptic patients, people who have had the God Experience simply *may not recall detail*. They do remember that at the time of the experience, the images seemed to be fixed forever. However, all they can remember now is "something" very significant happened.

The general property of egocentrism (Elhard 1968) within all of us perpetuates the sensation that the experience was real and unique. Since all of us feel we are somehow just a little more special than the other guy, such profound experiences are considered proofs of "selection." There are many illusions when personal experience is used as proof; they will be discussed in Chapter 5.

The profundity of God Experiences is evident by its consequences in human behavior. When they occur, people are convinced of their reality. The experience is so profound that people change their lives. External observers are impressed by the modifications and quickly point out that John Doe has become a new person since he found God, Yahweh, Allah, or the Cosmic Consciousness. The phrase may change but the theme remains the same.

One example of this behavioral modification was: "I had known Mr. S. for several years; he was a hateful and deceitful man. One day, he came to one of our meetings. He suddenly began to cry and begged us to pray for him. He sat there shaking and mumbling to himself and suddenly looked up and said that he had 'felt God touch his heart.' From that time on, he became a model citizen."

Perhaps the most dangerous aspect of this component of the God Experience is the extrapolation. Essentially, the logic goes like this: "I have had an experience with God; He has told me that I am His child. Whatever He tells me I must do, since He is the true Creator."

When this experience is manipulated by political groups or is contaminated by the individual's repressed wishes, the conviction can precipitate disaster. A person who has been punished or repressed by Jews may feel that "God wants all Jews punished," while another who thinks that the United States is the source of all trouble may feel that "in order to save the world, the United

States must be destroyed.'' These experiences are reported as real and profound. They give the person a sense of ''cosmic consent'' to kill and to manipulate others.

I cannot overemphasize the importance of the sense of conviction produced by these experiences. Following these small alterations in the temporal lobe, the person becomes convinced that what he or she has experienced is *absolutely right*. No amount of rational conversation or data can sway the opinion. The basic mentality appears to be, ''Once you're on the side of God, anything He says goes.''

The fine precision required to solve complex problems is lost in the crude emotion of the conviction. Alternative explanations are never seriously considered (although lip-service may be given otherwise). All decisions become simple-minded, all-or-none propositions; something is either right or wrong, spirit or matter, good or evil.

The profound component of the God Experience can become homicidal when paired with aggression. Uncontrolled, aggressive outbursts are associated with some types of temporal lobe epilepsy (Pontius 1984). To some extent, aggressive themes and behaviors are also expected in the God Experience.

Stories in the Old Testament, for example, are rife with instances of slaughter. In the name of Jehovah, masses of people were ''smited'' (even though the land belonged to them). During periods of killing, God Experiences were reported. Accounts were given of these ancient soldiers, grinning and killing with the enthusiasm and conviction of the God Experience (Trawick 1963).

Even the described behavior of Jehovah (Allah runs a close second) is typified by aggression and catastrophe. Punishment and death are evident in accounts of the flood and the indiscriminate destruction of ''enemies.'' In one famous instance, Jehovah became irritated at the Children of Israel because they were complaining about the same old food, so he sent quail until they had more than enough. One-quarter of the population allegedly died from contaminations in the quail. Whether the story is true or was intended to punish complainers is beside the point; intense bouts of aggression can be part of the God Experience.

Personal God Experiences also contain aggressive components. Instead of blatant rage or attack, the aggression may be more subtle and appear as a voice, impulse, or command. For example, Abraham, with the conviction of the God Experience, was going to kill his son, when at the last minute he was ''told'' otherwise. That was a few thousand years ago.

In 1979, a poor carpenter woke in the middle of the night and heard God's voice say that he should kill his four-month-old son. The man smashed in his son's skull with a hammer, convinced that he had been instructed by God to do so. Whereas this behavior may have been considered an act of faith a few hundred years ago, the contemporary jury was less impressed.

A second major cluster of symptoms in the God Experience includes the auditory and vestibular components. Since the temporal lobe contains the projection areas for the experience of hearing and the sensation of movement, transients within this portion of the brain should be predominated by auditory or vestibular experiences (Weingarten, Cherlow, and Holmgren 1977). No doubt these experiences could contain visual, olfactory, or taste images. Their presence would depend on how far the TLT spreads into other parts of the brain.

Next to "feeling the presence of God," "hearing God" is probably the most common mode of experience. The analogue of the sensation is the experience of having one's name called just before you fall asleep or of "hearing things" during periods of excessive fatigue. All of these sensations suggest the involvement of the temporal lobe.

"Hearing" or "feeling-hearing" the call of God is an extraordinarily common reference in most holy books. Prophets in the Bible, for example, "heard God's voice" speak within them, much like the hearing sensations of the epileptic. It is apparent that, like the temporal epileptic person, they could distinguish the difference between an "internal voice" and sounds from more routine external sources.

The attribution of the cause of the "voice" or sound varies markedly across cultures and throughout history. When Samuel heard his name called several times, the event was interpreted as the voice of God. Today, the call of a name is more likely to be considered a form of hypnogogic imagery produced during theta rhythm dominance in the temporal lobe. Even in a more secular light, the experience is still quite impressive.

Most "voice" displays of the God Experience are interpreted as a "whisper." The person just "knows" that the voice is God's. Like the epileptic aura, the word experiences are short sequences. Typical "heard sensations" are "Be still" or "Be still and know," which simply reiterates the *familiarity* component of the TLT.

Few people appear to acknowledge the role of vestibular sensations in the God Experience. However, in light of the temporal lobe's role in the sensation of balance and movement, these experiences are expected. Whereas the temporal lobe epileptic experiences crude sensations of movement, such as sudden feelings of rising (like going over a rolling road surface while riding in a car), or loss of orientation, the TLTs of religious experience are more subtle.

Literature concerned with the God Experiences are full of metaphors describing essential vestibular inputs. Sensations of "being lifted," "feeling light," or even "spinning, like being intoxicated," are common. A more general experience of ascension is flying or leaving the body.

God Experience involving temporal lobe instability is sometimes associated with a medical operation:

> Suddenly I felt myself being lifted up, like the movement in an elevator. I felt like I was moving down a long narrow corridor—I could see my body slowly moving away from "me." I was spinning around and around in the soft darkness. Then I stopped, it was like floating. At first I felt terror, then I heard a voice and all the fear left. The

voice said, "Go back, it's not yet your time," and *I knew* it was God. I did not want to return; the feeling of infinite peace was all around me and I hated to return to the pain of my life. Finally, I felt myself being tugged back into myself and I awoke. I knew I had felt the presence of God.

This account, often placed under the general rubric of "out-of-body experience" or "mystical interlude" is a classic form of depersonalization involving the temporal lobe (Persinger 1984b). Note the repeated references to vestibular sensations: "floating," "lifted," "moving," "spinning," and to the auditory experience, which was identified as God's voice. Commensurate with temporal lobe function was the experience of intense meaning. The person just knew the voice was familiar—it was the voice of God.

As in temporal lobe epilepsy (Gloor et al. 1982), some God Experiences are expected to have visual components. The person may find himself or herself in a distant place or merely have odd images superimposed on the real world. Visual experiences are frequently brief. Longer periods of intense visual experiences due to temporal lobe instability are frequently correlated with convulsions or blackouts. The reality of the event as a God Experience is more likely to be challenged in this century if convulsions occur.

Secondary properties of the God Experience reflect behaviors associated with normal variations in temporal lobe activity. Circumstantiality, obsession-compulsion, sobriety, specific euphoria, and widening of affect are the most typical symptoms (Bear and Fedio 1977; Geschwind 1983). Each of these will be defined and discussed briefly.

Circumstantiality is defined in this text as excessive persistence within a topic. The person who displays this behavior may inundate the observer with trivial details that seem to be exaggerated out of proportion. Coupled with this circumstantiality is viscosity, the tendency to stick to topics or to get "stuck" within a particular theme. Viscosity is most easily seen in the nature of the interpersonal action—the person talks and talks despite the many and often not-so-subtle social cues that the conversation is finished.

Obsession-compulsion is the label applied to repeated patterns of motor, word, or thought sequences. A simple example is the experience of having a song "playing over and over again in your head." At the level of the God Experience, obsession-compulsion is manifested as ritual. Typical rituals involve word sequences such as prayer. Body movements include playing with beads, kneeling on mats, or simple bobbing motions.

Sobriety is another component. Although some groups argue that the God Experience is elating, the event is not open to humor. The big grins and hearty enthusiasm about the spirit are shown only when the basic reality of the experience is assumed. If the experience is directly challenged by humor, the result is sobering.

The specific euphoria of the God Experience is very similar to intermediate levels of mania. The person feels more confident, full of life, and brimming with vigor. Clever manipulators use this "conversion energy" to continue the goals of the organization. With the energy of conversion, ordinary people have built churches and pounded the pavement to spread the word.

One of the interesting side effects of this component is induction by talking. If the God Experience has been very recent, the mere discussion of the topic can induce pleasurable shivering and flashbacks (much like certain hallucinogens). As time passes, the experience is remembered with a tone of soft security.

Widening of affect refers to the interpretation of everyday trivial circumstances as a part or proof of the God Experience. Natural fluke events, such as the conjunction of planets, the stopping of a clock, or the appearance of a butterfly, may be considered signs of the God Experience. In classical times, odd rainbows, earthquakes, and volcanoes were frequently given "meaning" in context of the God Experience.

The primary difference between the widened affect of the normal God Experience and that of the psychotic patient is one of degree (Buckley 1981). Temporal lobe psychotics incorporate more bizarre and trivial events into the God Experience (Slater and Beard 1963). For example, tooting of a car horn may be considered "proof" that the person is a child of God, or the color of the nurse's dress may imply that God has spoken. In one instance, a psychotic patient with clear temporal lobe overtones felt that he was a young fetus that had to kick three times and then be born again as Christ (Valliant 1982).

A reliance on *numbers* of mundane events or responses is especially typical of *group* God Experiences. Traditionally, the behaviors have included: walking a few times around the walls of a city in order for it to collapse, casting objects a fixed number of times on water (to get goodies), or calling three times into the grave of a dead man. Considering the role of the *temporal subcortex* in the sensation of meaningfulness, almost anything could obtain cosmic significance (Bear 1979).

The pairing of fear (real or hidden) with more intense God Experiences is expected. Fear and terror, in addition to the effects of the unusual experience, are frequent parts of the temporal lobe epileptic experience. In the God Experience, fear impulses induce the trembling, weak knees, and dry mouth typical of excessive emotional activity. Cries for mercy are also common.

Fear could contribute to submissive behaviors, such as falling onto the knees. This response affects the tone of the muscles of the legs. Submission rituals can be found in any human culture, whether the god is associated with terror or with good.

Crying commonly accompanies the emotional highs of the God Experience. While on their knees, people cry and sometimes sob and smile with exuberation during the peak of the TLT. One might expect the intensity of the God Experience to increase with more intense sobbing and submission.

Discussion of the contribution of temporal lobe properties to general themes in the God Experience cannot be concluded without some reference to dreams.

The experience of dreaming is intimately tied to the function of the temporal lobe (primarily) because of the hippocampus–amygdala complex. These portions of the brain receive fibers from the control areas for sleep and dreaming that are located in the brainstem.

The relationship between dreams and the God Experience is evident in almost any human culture studied. Human beings say they talk to gods through dreams, receive revelations through reveries, and predict the future through premonitions. Stimulation of the temporal lobe region can unleash dreamlike experiences over which the person has little control (Stevens 1982). Dream production can be induced directly by electrical peculiarities or by interfering with the chemical transmitters that effectively connect the neurons of the brain. Certain drugs appear to induce dreams during the waking state, when they may be experienced as real. All human cultures have developed some form of meditational technique to enhance the experience.

The properties of dreaming are heavily influenced by contributions of input from the adjacent brain structures. At the time of the dream, the actual experience may be associated with intense meaning. The dreamer may feel that he has found *the* answer to the universe or can understand some ancient writings. When the dreamer awakes and looks at the dream content without the accompanying amygdaloid seizures, the experience is trivial, sometimes even nonsensical.

All of us have had the experience; it's normal. A graduate student (in psychology) reported an excellent example of this pattern:

> One night I had a wonderful dream. I was standing near Christ on the Mount of Olives. Many other people were standing around as well. Suddenly, a cloud appeared over Christ's head and the people ran back in terror. Just before he began to rise into the sky, I ran up to him and got caught in some kind of force beam. I remember looking down upon the faces of the people below me as I moved further and further away. Suddenly, I looked up into the clouds and saw a spaceship, with the sides slowly opening, like the side doors of a helicopter. As I moved up towards it, being carried by the same force as Christ, I saw they were aliens. The next thing I remember is being on the ship and seeing Christ standing there. He smiled, and slowly took off his mask like on Mission Impossible. He was an alien too! He then turned to the others and said, "That should condition them."
>
> Then suddenly, they saw me standing there. I was told to go back onto the earth but that I would be guarded by a special piece of knowledge. At that moment, I woke up, wide awake and quickly grabbed some paper from the desk beside my bed and wrote it down. It said, "Propriety is the propensity for procreation."

The Old Testament is particularly revealing about the relationship between dreams and God Experiences. Although Biblical heroes did not rise on a force field to a spaceship, comparable vestibular and visual experiences were reported. One of the more well-known examples is Jacob, who dreams about climbing (moving) up a bright, golden ladder.

The relationships between God Experiences and dreams and between dreams and prophesy produce an interesting trinity. Attempts to peer into the future by searching tea leaves, animal entrails, or the esoteric symbols of the book of Revelation are perennial obsessions (especially during times of strife). Precise knowledge has one great attraction: If something can be predicted, there is no uncertainty; if there is no uncertainty, then there is no anxiety.

The very nature of dreams has predisposed them to being paired with prediction. Although dreaming is actually related to the processes of memory storage, the details of which we dream involve trivia. This is probably due to the modes of input to the temporal lobe; it receives information from a variety of indirect sensory routes. As a result, dream material contains subtleties that we usually ignore in the waking environment. Dreams contain indirect information that is picked up through peripheral vision or during periods when "concentration" is very low. When processed appropriately, these daily trivia can lead to accurate predictions that could not be obtained by more rational processes.

The mechanism by which the peripheral details of the day are coordinated is not clear, mostly because it has not been studied as systematically as more "logical" procedures. People with the proclivity (but not necessarily the accuracy) to make predictions based on dreams show a special kind of suggestibility. They pick up tidbits of information the way a sponge absorbs water. Always, though, there is an implied tincture of the God Experience.

The above descriptions of the components of the God Experience are more common to most cultures in some form. Remember, however, that God Experiences lie along a continuum. Only the TLTs are associated with the average kind of God Experience. At the more extreme levels of temporal lobe stimulation, motor components enter the picture (Goldensohn 1983; Stevens et al. 1969).

In the gray area between passive God Experience and the active seizure lies a mixture of the pathological and the profound. These God Experiences are associated with silly smiles (almost grimaces), periods of amnesia (during which the person talks in gibberish), active jumping or hopping, excessive salivation (or drooling), and a great deal of lip smacking and head jerking.

The gibberish is often called "speaking in tongues" and resembles the sounds emitted from young infants during the babbling stage. Since several portions of the brainstem control the movements of the voice box, the fact that the person is "unaware" of the experience is not a proof that a miracle has happened. Even organized speech can occur without "awareness."

God Experiences correlated with body movements are more intense and more violent than passive cases. During the euphoria, the person may become ballistic and throw his or her arms around, jump from side to side, and sometimes cause injury.

The severity of the temporal lobe transient can be inferred by the fragmented or total memory loss of particular episodes. During the height of the excitement, when the person is "possessed by the spirit—be it human, Holy or animal form,'' the person is totally dissociated. Although he or she may respond to commands, the event is not recalled. Sometimes, if they are clever, these people infer what has happened or pay attention to the verbal cues of people talking with them after the episode.

Behaviors manifested during the dissociated states are related to the particular culture. The specific responses reflect a combination of repressed wishes (which reflect the society) and the expectations of the situation. Not surprisingly, these God Experiences may occur with bright visual hallucinations and occasional convulsions. Even without a convulsion, the person shows muscle weakness or tiredness for several hours afterward.

Psychological addiction to this type of God Experience occurs because of the brain's chemical reaction to the intense motor agitation or to the seizure. The release of the brain's own opiates can cause a narcotic high during the agitation; as might be expected, special receptors for these opiates are found within the amygdala. Elevation of brainstem levels of norepinephrine elevate mood for several days to weeks. The person can become addicted not only to the God Experience but to the *God high*.

Few groups of people in Western culture accentuate or emphasize this type of God Experience. Symptoms of this more dangerous God Experience can be found in some Pentecostal and Southern Baptist groups. Modern bizarre movements also show this trend. Very agitated components of the God Experience are much more common in African cultures and in radical Moslem believers.

Prediction of when and where God Experiences will occur depends on one essential factor, temporal lobe stability. Any condition that precipitates TLTs can result in the God Experience. Since the temporal lobe is very sensitive to changes in hypoxia (lack of oxygen), blood sugar (hypoglycemia), and blood flow, situations that produce these symptoms are most correlated with the God Experiences.

The most common source of hypoxia (outside of frank suffocation) is high altitudes. At the heights of tall mountains or high plateaus, the oxygen tension of the air begins to approach the bare requirements for normal function. Although one can ultimately adjust to these hypoxic environments, significant alterations in temporal lobe activity occur during the interim. Many ancient religious figures were known to climb to the tops of mountains. Upon these heights, religious experiences took place. God spoke to the listener and gave special messages.

A second source of hypoxia is associated with low-level breathing. Maintained yoga breathing episodes, if the person is trained appropriately, can drive the temporal lobe into bouts of theta activity. Sometimes frank electrical seizures will occur, and the God Experience is reported.

As the person learns to induce (and to control) TLTs through meditation, the God Experience becomes enhanced by vestibular sensations. The person may experience the illusion of levitation or simple ''rising.'' ''Jerks'' in selected leg muscles might also occur in more extreme conditions.

Hypoxia, although a popular stimulation source among meditational groups, is far less attractive than hypoglycemia for the production of God Experiences. Many Western and non-Western cultures alike have developed varied techniques of starvation in order to obtain the God Experience.

Young initiates among American Indian tribes were required to starve themselves until a God Experience occurred. It was usually described as a contact with a spirit guide, such as a totem or animal form. Although the details were determined by cultural expectations, the general profundity of the God Experience was present. This single event influenced the person's life from then on.

Wandering through the wilderness and quasi-starvation were popular Biblical techniques for obtaining the God Experience. Most communications with Jehovah (or Satan) occurred during protracted periods of effective starvation. Fasting was a less intense method. All of these techniques assume, of course, that the person has had a more or less adequate diet previous to the fast.

In twentieth century Western culture, few people purposely starve themselves or deprive themselves of oxygen. However, there are other methods that bring about optimal deviations in the temporal lobe. They include major operations (when the blood flow decreases) and periods of fever. For example, one young person who had a severe case of scarlet fever reported:

> As I drifted in and out of consciousness, I felt I was going to die. Then suddenly I heard a voice say, "Don't worry, I am with you." I looked up and saw a soft white ray coming through the window. The voice said, "I am the Christ, through me there is salvation." I knew I had seen God. I was no longer afraid. When I awoke, my mother told me that two days had passed.

The most common condition that facilitates the God Experience is personal stress (Clark 1958). *Stress* is a vague term, but in this instance, I am referring to physiological stress. This type of stress is associated with elevations of chemicals like ACTH (adrenocorticotrophic hormone) from the pituitary, the corticosteroids, and other hormones produced by the endocrine organs of the human body.

These chemicals are disturbed during sudden and maintained changes in life style. Moderate changes in life style include leaving home, moving to a new city, attending university, starting a new job, or even taking a vacation. It makes no difference whether these changes are "good" (a promotion) or "bad" (being fired). The important factor is the *change*.

More severe changes in life style include divorces, middle-age crises, career failures, and most of all, death of a loved one. Death of very close people, especially those that compose a major portion of the daily life ritual, have devastating effects on the body's physiology. Suddenly, when these people die, the whole world falls apart. Their deaths produce sudden and maintained changes in the life style of the survivor.

Death, although always a serious event, varies with respect to the relative impact on the person. Women whose entire life centered around their husbands are more adversely affected by becoming widows than are women who also had a career. Although both types of women lose their husbands, the woman with the career has had other structures in her life.

One special type of life-style change is the loss of children, not from death, but from maturity. Although not publicized as well as the consequences of death, the sudden removal of a mother's children from her midst is a severe life-style change. If a woman has identified herself throughout adult life as "a mother," the sudden loss of her last child results in a terrible crisis. Now she feels she is no longer anything or anybody.

The elevation of the stress hormones have both direct and indirect effects on the hippocampus, amygdala, and other portions of the temporal lobe (Feldman and Paul 1976). These chemicals have been shown to contribute to memory storage (and may even influence the sequence of how we remember things) by directly influencing temporal lobe structures. Under these conditions, fantasies can be stored as actual memories; it is difficult to tell the difference after the experience is stored.

These hormones also produce indirect effects on the hippocampus and related structures by decreasing the amount of serotonin in the brainstem. This chemical (an important transmitter in the brain) is associated with the onset of sleep and is frequently less concentrated in the brainstem during periods of elevated stress hormone activity. Maintained low levels of serotonin (and norepinephrine or noradrenalin) are correlated with depression and suicidal impulses.

A common correlate with depressed levels of serotonin in the brainstem is the sudden occurrence of dream sleep in other states of consciousness. This experience of dreams during waking and especially borderline states occurs as the system becomes almost exhausted. From the depths of the sense of loss, vivid and realistic dream images can burst into awareness.

In general, the more severe the disturbance, the more intense the God Experience. The most profound God Experiences occur after the sudden loss (death) of a close loved one. Most of them occur within one to four days of the death of the individual and are coincident with an experience of the dead person appearing, smiling, and testifying that God is there. Interestingly, few details are usually remembered, although a definite sense of communion or communication is retained. The person "knows" that the person is with God.

Sometimes details are "recalled." One interesting example (and there are estimated to be hundreds of thousands of reports every decade) is the following:

> When Fred died, the world collapsed around me. I could not eat or sleep, everything seemed to lose its color—food was tasteless, I couldn't swallow because of this lump in my throat; it would not go away no matter how much I cried. My mental pain would come and go like chill waves. Sometimes I would forget for a few minutes and think it was all a bad dream. Other times, the reality of it would hit me like a cold shower. The fourth night after he died, I lay in bed, trying to piece my life together. I lay there for

hours. Suddenly, I felt Fred's presence beside me in the bed. I looked over and saw him standing beside me. He was dressed in his old work clothes and had a big smile on his face. He said "Don't worry Maud. I'm in heaven now. God has let me come to you. All our friends are here too. It's all true, what we believed about God. . . . this is only a temporary separation." I went to sleep and didn't wake for hours. The next day I felt good, the sun was shining again; there was meaning to my life. No matter what you say, Dr. Persinger, I know that God exists because I have experienced His presence.

The intense physiological upheaval following the death of a loved one is clearly seen in this case history. Emotional flatness, lumps in the throat, loss of taste, and the wavelike fluctuations of grief and incapacitation are typical. In this instance, the God Experience occurred during the early morning hours following several "sleepless" nights and almost no (recalled) dreaming.

The experience indicates temporal lobe involvement. First there is the wish component of normal dreams. The experience confirms old expectations about where "dead friends go" and supports the belief about heaven. Then there is the "meaningfulness" of the event. Whereas before the experience, the person was incapable of dealing with the environment, afterward she could plan and prepare for the future. In short her life, due to a single temporal lobe transient, was "real" once more.

Considering the general nature of death and its consequences for the living, God Experiences should occur in every culture and throughout human time. The basic themes have not changed because the behavioral operation (the sudden removal of a person with whom all types of complicated associations have been made) and the *construction* of human brains have been the same for thousands of years! Cross-cultural and historical data confirm these comments (Clark 1958; Leslie 1960).

However, the actual details (the facts that are so important to the individual's sense of proof) should vary and do vary with the experience; these have changed across space and time. Over the centuries, God Experiences associated with death have shifted from golden gates and lands of milk and honey to "garden concepts." A most recent trend (among secular young people) is a type of other dimension–infinity idea.

People who still interpret the Bible literally or whose only religious training occurred in childhood, still report the "garden and heaven" concept. Repeated reports of these experiences for centuries may not reflect the absolute nature of the experiences. Instead, it may reflect the fact that people have been reading the *same* material.

Less intense life-style changes such as children moving away from home, can also lead to a God Experience. Depending on the degree of hormonal arousal and the instability of the temporal lobe, the experience can occur due to simple cumulative effects. They are less spectacular, per se, but just as impressive and meaningful to the person.

For example, one 50-year-old woman felt that she had lost all her energy. She became tired easily and just didn't care about anything anymore. She would sit for long hours in front of the TV set and wonder what her children were doing. Her last child had left home for university just a few months before. Then one night, she reported:

> I was sitting by myself beside the fireplace; I couldn't sleep very well during the previous nights, something just didn't seem right. I thought about my life and what it was like when I was a child. Then there was an odd sensation and I felt as if my heart had been embraced. The warmest experience I had ever felt touched me and I knew that God was there.

The following Sunday, the individual went to a local church (the first time in years). Her mood became clearly elevated and she decided to paint the house. She became a member of a local humanity group and an active churchgoer. With this new structure in her life, meaning emerged again.

There are a variety of drugs that can precipitate God Experiences. Although they work through the same chemical mechanisms that produce spontaneous God Experiences, drug modes are more suspect in Western culture. In fact, many religious sects make a clear distinction between the "true" or spontaneous God Experience and those induced by chemicals. When the transcripts of both types of experiences are compared, the basic *themes* are the same.

Some cultures place significant emphasis on "mind-bending" drugs in order to reach God. Most of the chemicals, such as mescaline, peyote, and LSD derivatives, influence the chemical systems directly associated with the temporal lobe. Each drug produces slightly different and unique experiences, depending on its pharmacological properties.

Acute or sudden displays of the God Experience can be precipitated by any number of auditory or vestibular inputs. The most typical auditory input is music. Music has the interesting capability to stimulate not only the temporal lobe but other portions of the brain as well. In fact, because of this capability, singing and music can facilitate speech in patients who typically cannot speak in full sentences.

The effects of music on emotions are well documented. Appropriate patterns of music can induce quiescence and relaxation, while other sequences can induce sexual and aggressive impulses. Mood manipulation by music is a common technique for "preparing" a crowd (whether they be in a church or at a rock concert) for the message to follow.

During periods of physiological instability and temporal lobe transients, music can be tightly coupled with emotions. Later, when the person grows up, the presentation of an old song releases all types of old, vivid emotional memories. The heart pounds and awareness drifts as the adult suddenly finds himself or herself reminiscing, with tears in the eyes or a lump in the throat, about the "good old days." There is less anxiety in the good old days; there is no uncertainty; it has already happened.

The importance of the temporal lobe itself rather than the actual pattern of the sounds for emotional memories is evident by the great variety of music that can induce similar effects. To the person who listened to the songs of Benny Goodman and Harry James, the sounds of rock and roll are ineffective stimuli. To another, who grew up during the time of Elvis Presley or The Supremes, contemporary sounds are only so much noise.

Music can trigger the occurrence of TLTs in the sensitive brain. According to the reports of people who "feel the hand of God" or "are moved by the spirit," the experience is paired mostly with episodes of song. Musical stimuli presented after sermons or messages that are full of colorful and emotional metaphors, are especially effective for unleashing the God Experience.

The potency of music in precipitating a God Experience is evident from simple inspection. Adult men and women, who have maintained an objective and clear evaluation of the world around them, suddenly break into tears. Their legs shake (some fall to their knees) and their heart pounds. At the same time, they experience the high, a sense of relief ("of burdens being lifted") and a deep sense of quiescence.

Very loud music or sound patterns can drive the epileptic brain into bouts of seizure. TLTs can also be influenced by very loud music, especially if it is interspersed with sharp sounds such as clapping or vocalization ("Amen" or "Allah"). Some of the most successful God Experience procedures involve groups of people singing, clapping, and screaming. They are very important components of revivals and of group "feelings," such as Catholic masses and Moslem meditations.

Sounds have traditionally been important precipitators of the God Experience in non-Western cultures. Repetitive sounds, such as those produced by water falls, the wind blowing through the treetops, or the waves of water on the beach have been designated as "areas of spirits." In such sounds people from myriad cultures have "heard" the whispers and calls of spiritual creatures.

The importance of vestibular sensations as a component of the God Experience has been mentioned. Because the temporal lobe receives input from parts of the brain that allow the experience of balance or movement, this is not surprising. It is also predictable that excessive or appropriate movement of the body can precipitate or enhance the God Experience.

The types of body movements associated with God Experience are as varied as human culture. Body movements take the form of swaying, dancing, bobbing forward and backward, bowing, or jumping. The critical feature is the monotony and rhythm of the movement that increases the tempo until it reaches some maximum value.

Ritual dancing is frequently cited as an important portion of the God Experience. Singing, chanting, and dancing are abundant in African cultures. Except for the very animated religious groups in North America, such as some Southern Baptists, Pentecostal sects, and borderline cults, body movements are not emphasized in North America.

The sense modality that is least manipulated (to our knowledge) in Western culture to precipitate or to accentuate the God Experience is smell. Like epileptic seizures, certain smells should be able to precipitate the God Experience. Perfumes, incense, and other aromatic compounds are examples. The temporal lobe is the "home" of olfaction.

A final feature in the prediction of the biological factors contributing to God Experiences is the individual stability of the temporal lobe. A variety of idiosyncratic factors influence temporal lobe stability. They include birth traumas, mechanical damage (concussions) during development, degenerative diseases, hormonal fluctuations, and the development of scleroses.

Recent research indicates that although people with relatively small or poorly developed temporal lobes are more likely to show abnormalities, a more important aspect is the degree of nerve growth in the lobe. Areas with few nerve endings are more prone to electrical instability (Haracz 1984). Lack of growth often is determined by failures in blood supply due to disease or trauma.

A second, well-documented factor associated with temporal lobe instability is the fusion of cell membranes. The temporal lobe has a tendency to contain neurons and other (glial) cells whose membranes are fused together. Consequently, when one neuron is stimulated, large numbers of others are also fired. This does not typically happen in most portions of the brain where the neurons are more insulated.

The degree to which mechanical trauma or normal chemical changes during life cause these odd properties of the temporal lobe is not clear. However, they certainly contribute to instability. God Experiences should be statistically more likely to occur among people with early histories of concussions in the temporal region (but without seizures), during pregnancy, among populations with thiamine deficiency, and in brains with poor blood supply.

Chronologically, there should be two major peaks in the occurrence of the God Experience. The first peak in the population should be associated with the massive temporal lobe instability of adolescence. During early adolescence, expecially around puberty, temporal lobe electrical patterns appear that would be considered abnormal if they occurred in the adult population.

This temporal lobe component can be seen in the increased frequency of daydreaming and intermediate altered states that typify this age period. These partial dissociations are associated with the "dazed look" that almost epitomizes adolescent mentality. Occasionally, daydreaming is accompanied by a blank smile. In more extreme cases, there may also be bouts of amnesia. For example, the young person may walk into his room to find a toy and then forget why he went to the room in the first place.

From the period of pubescence to the later teens (and sometimes into the first part of the third decade), the growing individual displays significant physiological instability (or stress). The stress hormones are significantly elevated, compared to the later, stable periods of adulthood. Associated with this instability are the typical large mood swings of adolescence. The young person may plunge from euphoric enthusiasm to deep and suicidal depression when presented with the simplest of frustrations.

Typical questions asked during this period of life are: "What's it all about?" and "Isn't there something more to life?" These tip-of-the-tongue sensations are complemented by the questions of identity crisis, such as, "Who am I really?" or "What is reality?" If the sensation of self is influenced by inputs into the brain from all over the body, then the upheavals of adolescence should alter the feelings of "who I am." The sensation of self seems slippery and elusive; it's there but you can never grab it.

The second peak would occur among the aged. This would be increased if sclerotic diseases (disorders of blood circulation due to narrowing or "clogging" of the blood vessels) occurred. As the temporal lobe in general and the hippocampus in particular were deprived of more and more blood supply by the slow sclerotic progression, the number and the intensity of TLTs would increase.

Of course, the effect would be U-shaped. In other words, too much damage to the hippocampus and surrounding tissues would produce massive loss of function. The God Experience would be unlikely in a brain prone to periods of dead silence. God Experiences would be evident during the earlier stage of degeneration that is characterized by spike and slow waves, in the Electroencephalogram.

Electroencephalographic abnormalities, consisting of slow waves and sharp waves over the temporal areas of the brain, have been observed in 30-40 percent of an apparently normal elderly sample (Reitan and Wolfson 1985). Under the age of 40 years, the incidence of this type of EEG pattern is only about 3 percent. As would be expected (Bear and Fedio 1977), the foci of the electrical lability in the elderly is in the left anterior temporal lobe in about 80 percent of the cases. The concern for personal destiny and the orientation towards God Beliefs should permeate subjective experience.

On the basis of some very general properties of the temporal lobe, a few testable statements about the *nature* of the God Experience have been made. By knowing the conditions that precipitate TLTs, you can predict when or where the God Experience could occur.

However, one pressing question remains. Why does the God Experience contain such a persistent "origin" theme? Why is the image of the God Experience full of childlike metaphors, such as "being born again"? Why is the basic question involved with "Who am I and where am I going?" The obsession with nascence themes can be seen especially among temporal lobe patients (Bear and Fedio 1977).

In the context of the present hypothesis, there must be some feature of the temporal lobe that is involved with the experience or origin of the self-concept.

This feature must be a normal aspect of the brain's growth from the fetal, infant, and early childhood stages into adulthood.

The adult's sense of "body image" is associated primarily with the parietal lobe. This cortex, which is slightly above the temporal lobe, receives information from all the parts of the body. We learn that the arms, legs, and internal responses are a part of the body boundary, the thing each of us calls the self.

Adults who have damage to this part of the brain experience a fragmentation of their body image. Depending on where the damage occurred, the person may feel that his arm no longer belongs to him or that he has no body from the legs down. These people may find the continued appearance of their limbs to be alarming (much the way you would feel if a chair followed you around).

That is a property of the adult brain. But, for the first few months of life, the body image is not totally associated with the parietal lobe. Instead, it appears to be "stored" in the temporal lobe. During the time when the new being is dependent on the behaviors of the mother and father and the *pattern* of those behaviors, the temporal lobe integrates and grows with that information.

During the first few years of life, when the baby spends a significant portion of its sleep in the dream phases, the early thoughts and images of consciousness are strengthened or weakened by the way the mother and father respond. First, the body image and then the sense of self begin to emerge. I hypothesize that this transient involvement of the temporal lobe with those twilight times of life determines the nascence themes of the God Experience. It is from this information that the vague experiences of diffuse origin will ultimately emerge.

Normally, these experiences are locked away. As the person matures, other parts of the brain become involved and the role of the temporal lobe shifts to other functions. The old memories are forgotten. But they are there, ready to be released by the appropriate key. That key is the temporal lobe transient. When it occurs, the images and protosensations long locked within the old contexts of the temporal lobe are released. The adult experiences the old sense of the infant self to which he or she has not had access for decades.

But it is not a pure experience; instead, it is mixed and merged with the experiences of a lifetime. These old themes are felt within the contexts of the adult perception. Infinity is not the boundary of the crib, but the end of the universe. Eternity is not the few seconds to the next suckle of warm milk, but the extent of all adult time.

Basic images, long forgotten, are retrieved during the God Experience. However, the most fundamental theme, persistent throughout all human existence because of the very nature of the human being, is the relationship between the child and the parent. For it is during these earlier years that the infantile sense of self is permanently shaped and bound to the patterns of parental behavior. Predictably, these patterns will be hidden within the unlimited details of adult learning, in the God Experience.

4
Egocentrism: The Power Behind the Proof

The conviction with which a person believes in the validity and infallibility of the God Experience or Concept is a consequence of the power of the egocentric reference. Each of us is self-centered. Even the altruist, who allegedly behaves for the sake of others, is still personally rewarded for his or her ''good'' deeds.

Egocentrism is not necessarily correlated with arrogance or extroversion. Quiet, humble people can be just as egocentric as the most abrasive braggart. *Egocentrism* refers to the relative reliance placed on one's personal experience as a proof of reality.

Dependence on the egocentric reference is fostered by emotional immaturity and an adoration for the ''innocence'' of a child's mentality. Emphasis on ''having the faith of a child'' encourages the selfish contention that there is absolutely no reason to question experiences or beliefs. They simply are because they were experienced.

Neither intelligence nor education necessarily weans us from this destructive type of thinking. Advanced degrees or clever manipulations of words cannot make up for a lack of psychological maturity. This only comes when one's deepest personal experiences are challenged against the objectivity of emotionless data when we see ourselves for what we are, outside the egocentric reference.

Within the power of egocentric reference, all of us assume that our experiences are real and true (Browning 1968). We presume our memories to be accurate representations of what has happened. We assume that if we perceive something, it must exist; or, if we have not experienced something, it does not exist.

Individuals place great significance on the importance of their personal experience. It is used as proof of probationary phenomena merely because ''I have experienced it." How many times have you heard a phrase like "I believe in God [UFOs, or whatever] because I have experienced it." Conversely, how many times have you heard the statement like "Baah, UFOs [or God, or whatever] do *not* exist because I have *not* experienced them." There is always that dependence on the persistent "I."

The average person will defend, sometimes to death, the validity of personal experience. Before he or she contends that the experience may have been an error, every piece of possible supporting evidence will be offered to demonstrate the proof. Against data, social opinion, and sometimes direct confrontation that the experience was a lie, people will still persist about in validity of their own perceptions.

If people understand the arbitrary nature of their experience, they would panic. If people realized the instability of their memories, especially about emotional events, the sense of mastery would be shattered. With experience unsure and memory unstable, the sense of self (who you are and where you are going) would be indicted. The panic and the terror would be intolerable.

The average person must believe in the absolute nature of at least *some experiences*, especially those that are identified with the definition of personal being. A person must be convinced that he or she is somehow a little more special than all others. He or she must contend that these personal experiences are as absolute as the eternity of time and the infinity of space.

There is nothing closer to the basic conception of self than the God Experience. Because of the construction of the human brain (Chapters 2 and 3) and the intimate intermingling of the first personal concepts with parental patterns (Chapter 6), the God Experience lies at the root of personal experience. To question it is to question the validity of the self. Few people can do this and survive.

One professor of biology, who is also an ardent member of a pentecostal church, aptly summarized this common human theme. He stated,

> I know that people believe in God in different ways and I am compelled to allow them to see God in the way they wish. I have read that other cultures have odd and bizarre means of worshiping God. But I know my own experiences must be true. Other people talk about the Holy Spirit whenever they are sick, depressed or just helpless. But I know my own experiences must be true; they cannot be simple flukes in my brain.

When asked about the contradiction between his training as a scientist and his personal belief, his answer contained an unusual and extraordinarily revealing evaluation. Although he later denied the sequence, he reported,

> If you are asking me do I believe in laying on the hands and the Spirit entering a group of people in prayer, of course I believe. How else could I help build a church in which we worship? Or go to the service every week? Or tell my children that God will

protect them forever? Of course God exists, for if He did not, which to me is inconceivable, how could Man survive? How could I survive now and forever after? What *meaning* would there be at all?

How does such power of the egocentric reference emerge? What is the source of the compelling feelings that our experiences are true? Where in the past does the individual achieve the capacity to place his or her personal God Experience above the reality and testability of continuous contradiction? Why is "my experience" just a little more real than all the others? The answer lies in two parts.

The first source of the egocentric reference is buried so deeply within human experience that it is rarely realized. Each human body is constructed to respond only to those stimuli (or environmental events) that impinge on the small volume of space that is called the "I" or "self." A person does not respond in the same way to stimuli that occur at a distance.

Although this description is common sense, the consequences are profound. True, we do not respond to that proverbial tree that falls in an isolated forest within Siberia. We do not respond to the death of a minute insect as it is squashed beneath one's heel. These are obvious.

As individuals, none of us responds directly to the hunger pains of the starving in the third world. We do not feel the pain of a black student as he is being beaten or shot by South African police. We don't experience the frustrations of the young ghetto black who revels in movie fantasy, but must then walk out into the cold reality of the street. We can *empathize* with how it may feel, if we saw or heard about those events, but we cannot feel them directly.

No matter how lucid the imagination, inference is never the same as direct stimulation. The distension of a swollen abdomen is painful only when it occurs within *your* body. The agony of violence is real only when it is happening to you. You are most likely to feel deep resentment and anger over discrimination when *you* are the victim.

There is a universe of difference between the direct consequences of human pain and the empathy of a bleeding heart. It is the difference between the stimuli that trigger the reflexes and the learned feelings that are the conditioned response to indirect experiences. Like words, the most common example of conditioned stimuli, they never have the total impact of the original stimuli.

The fact that each person is an island unto himself or herself is a biological consequence. It is the way our bodies are constructed. Our nerve nets do not expand deep into the great volume of the earth; they do not stretch across its surface. They do not overlap with the approximately four billion units that compose our small species. Instead, each of us responds to a small chunk of space that we learn to call "the body." Within the nerve nets of this little space, a matrix of stimuli is fused and formed. Slowly the concept of self is shaped.

Initially, as individuals, in those semiconscious years of infancy, we float in a dreamlike world. Space and time are fused together. As infants we lay in the crib or on our backs in confusion.

Each infant learns that certain stimuli, especially those of touch, pain, cold, warmth, and movement, are registered when they hit a certain point in space. The same hot bottle that did nothing a few inches from the little hand becomes a source of pain when it is touched. A pin that inertly held the diaper together becomes a prick when it is brought within the body space.

Slowly, the concept of the body boundary is shaped. The young infant learns that the wiggly appendages are the fingers and the pumping forms are the legs and feet. At first, the passage of the hand across the visual field is a strange event. It elicits a sense of surprise when he touches it and experiences the sensation of the body image. The hand belongs to him.

You learn that other people are different. Indeed, they, too, have hands and feet. But their movements are not felt by you. Other people are stuck by pins or burned by heat, but their pain is not experienced. Other people starve to death but their agony has no sensation.

Sure, even the young child will cry when it sees another child stuck by a pin or punished. However, these occur only if the child has *learned* that these stimuli are aversive. The conditioned stimuli, by themselves, are rarely as potent as those events that evoke effects without learning.

Because of this biological construction and the nature of human learning, we can see how every individual on this planet must feel that his or her experiences are somehow just a *little more real* than another's. Only the stimuli that influence the individual are remembered; those that influence everyone else can only be inferred.

For a brief moment, we can digress and speculate about what each human being might experience if each of us were connected to *everyone* else. Imagine how it would be if you directly felt (at the same time) the agony of the third world or the pain of the slum dweller. In today's world, with millions in pain and trepidation, each of us would live in constant agony.

At first, the individual nightmare would not end. But if we managed to pass that period without a nervous breakdown, how much starvation would be left in the world if each of us personally felt the pangs of another's malnutrition? How many wars would be fought if each of us experienced the searing pain of bullets ripping through our bodies as a young boy fell to his death in some distant rice paddy?

The concept of the human self would be markedly different. Since the experiences of every single element of the four billion forms that compose this species would flood your boundary every second of every day, you would no longer experience the conviction of a special or unique individual. The concept of self would reflect more than the limits of a nerve net within the small volume of a body. Indeed, a person would be a different thing.

Obviously, human experience does not operate in such a fashion. The small volume called the body is a "locus of behaviors" (Persinger 1980) that are constantly rewarded and maintained. Because this locus is the major region of individual experience, it achieves special properties.

There are many components in this locus of behavior. The most important for the sensation of egocentric references is the experience of self. Its properties include the report of consciousness, the recognition of being an individual, living thing, and the sensation of free will, the ability to control one's own destiny.

Immature people, no matter what the age, are dominated by the egocentric reference. It is most clearly seen in the child who assumes that his or her experiences are the only experiences. Some researchers have said that childhood can be seen as a preponderance of "I"s and paucity of "we"s.

When a child walks up to an adult and says; "Have you seen Jimmy?" there is an implicit assumption that only the child's Jimmy exists. When the adult says, "Jimmy who?" the child looks back with disbelief at the adult's unmitigated ignorance and says, "Why Jimmy Jones, who else?" To the young child, her experiences are the only experiences (and therefore must be evident to everyone else). She does not realize that there are thousands of Jimmys outside of her reference.

The intensity of the child's egocentric reference lingers into the adulthood of the uneducated and sheltered person. During World War II, when the beliefs of the day were tested in the number of battlefield kills, a normal looking adult woman ran up to a sailor and asked, "Have you seen Mark?" When the sailor said, "Mark who?" the woman replied, with some surprise, "Well Mark Wilson, of course." When the sailor said that he did not know the person, the woman returned with some surprise, "But, he's in the navy!" An adult body does not always mean adult thinking.

As people mature psychologically, the egocentrism wanes. The rare mature person does not see himself as special or unique. In fact, as he or she grows older, the egocentric illusion becomes obvious. Interestingly, the conviction about the validity of God Experiences and about other references totally dependent on personal experience become suspect as well.

One of the most reinforcing aspects of being a university professor is the look on the faces of first-year students when they realize that most of the experiences they thought were unique for so many years are shared by everyone else. At first, they look with disbelief; a few giggle. Some squirm uneasily because they think (as they report later) the only way I could have known was to have "read their minds."

Until this time, they had failed to realize that human experiences are *not* unique. They only appear unique because the individual does not have direct access to other people's private behaviors. Other people feel lumps in their throats when a loved one dies. Other people spend minutes thinking to themselves about what they should have said, after an argument has been lost. Other people also see blinks of light while lying in the dark, perceive floaters "moving in space" (when staring into diffuse light), and hear ringing in the ears.

When each student is given the *same* set of descriptions about his or her personality, each of them are flabbergasted by the accuracy. They are amazed that statements like "once in a while, you feel like you cannot cope with life" or "at times you feel nothing can go wrong" accurately describe their own behaviors. Each person thinks that it refers only to himself. The first time they learn that everyone received the same questions and each person felt the descriptions were "incredibly accurate," some students are clearly shaken.

One of the greatest lessons taught by psychology and behavioral analysis is that people are *not unique* in their basic experiences. They only *interpret* their experiences from an egocentric reference. Since they can compare their experiences only to their own existence, they have no other sets of comparison.

The egocentrism of existence is around us every day. It is built into the language with the constant references to "I" and "me" or "mine." Each of us refers to other people, but not as individuals with rights and privileges. Instead, people are things that are directly or indirectly ours: "my wife," "my children," "my father."

We see the world through egocentric glasses. Events that occur within our sphere of experience are given special reference. If a person from your town is killed in an automobile accident, the news is spread across the front pages of the local paper. People lament, close friends cry, and the family grieves.

On the other hand, suppose some distant, isolated island is obliterated by a tidal wave. Several thousand human beings, each with his or her own feelings of specialty and selection, die in a froth of sand and ocean. The event receives, perhaps, a small paragraph on the back page. It is outside of our experience, outside of our concern. To some people, it may not exist at all.

The world is like a giant ink-blot that reveals our egocentric references. If "my friend" talks in odd jargon then he must "be talking in tongues." If someone else from a small town in West Virginia speaks the very same way, it is merely a sign of brain disorder. If "my friend" hears his name called at night, then it is a deep experience. If a derelict on skid row hears the call, he is suffering a hallucination.

Egocentric reference reduces the recognition of "third factors"—events or explanations that are not seen because they have not been or cannot be directly experienced by the person. This inability to see "all the variables" makes the egocentric individual prone to superstitious associations. It is the second factor in the power of conviction.

The *principle of contiquity* is the fundamental basis of human learning (Hergenhahn 1982). Events that occur together in time are paired in such a way that the occurrence of one evokes the memory of the other. Some events are clearly maintained by their consequences, by what they produce. If every time you smile at a girl, she then looks in your direction, the likelihood that you will smile again is much stronger. If every time you scream, your husband pays attention, the likelihood you'll scream again (even louder) becomes greater.

Other responses are only accidentally associated with consequences. Although these responses do not deliver the actual rewards or punishments, they occur close together in space and time with positive or negative things. As a result, these responses also become more likely. This is called *superstitious learning*.

Our daily lives are filled with examples. Your cat sets quietly and stares at the door knob. Accidentally, you pass by and see the cat and let him into another room. Even though the cat's stares had nothing to do with the opening of the door (you opened the door), the posture is rewarded. The next time the cat may sit for hours, staring at the door knob, waiting.

Superstitious conditioning is often responsible for "misinterpretations" of relationships in nature. For example, one famous scientist thought that his thoughts could control the oxygen consumption of a potato plant. He took the potato plant into a small room and concentrated on it. Sure enough, after a few minutes, there was a change in the oxygen consumption of the plant. He concluded, "my thoughts have controlled the plant."

However, this was an example of superstitious conditioning. In fact, two things were occurring at the same time: (1) thinking and (2) his body was *also* using up oxygen within the small room. However, since he did not measure the oxygen consumption but only responded to his thoughts, he concluded that the thoughts were responsible. (Later experiments indicated that if the oxygen in the room was controlled, no amount of "concentration" would influence the potatoes.)

The most blatant case of superstitious conditioning is the famous "drowning man parable." During drowning, two types of behaviors are very likely: the first is swimming or some crude approximation. The second behavior is thinking. Since the situation is close to complete helplessness, the most likely theme is "God save me" or some crude approximation.

Ultimately, swimming around results in delivery of the reward, for example, the man grabs a log. Since the man is saved, the swimming has been rewarded. In a similar situation and at another time, he is very likely to swim toward a log again.

However, there was also another behavior going on at the time of the rescue: the thought "God save me." It was also rewarded because it was occurring at the time of the rescue. Even though the phrase had absolutely *nothing* to do with the rescue, the phrase is more likely to be repeated again. The person concludes, "God saved me!"

Now the punch line of this classic case demonstrates the power and lopsided nature of superstitious learning. The conclusion "God saved me" is only going to be stated by people who *survived* the ordeal. Those individuals who also thought "God saved me" and who *drowned* are not around to tell the difference.

The determination of whether or not a response has been superstitiously acquired can be a bit tricky. In the above situation, the person would have to go back into the situation and think, "God save me" without swimming. If he were saved, then the conclusion could be made that the thoughts were responsible for the rescue. Few people have such empirical courage.

In a similar way, the feelings of mastery over the universe could be shaped within the young infant. It would start simply, probably accidentally, as a part of human life. Sometimes, during that twilight state of early consciousness, the child lies waiting for the next bottle to arrive. He experiences a thought (let's call it a protothought, some early semblance of what will later be called private responses to thinking). The parent cannot experience the thought but the infant does not realize this limit. He waits; nothing happens. The food deprivation takes its toll and hunger reaches some critical value.

Then the child cries out and suddenly the mother appears with a bottle. The infant sucks and the hunger subsides. As a result of this consequence, the bringing of the milk, two things are likely to happen again. The first response is the crying, the event to which the mother responded. The second response is the one to which she did not respond: the protothought. It, too, was reinforced, even though technically it has absolutely *nothing* to do with the delivery of the milk.

With each sequence of protothought, crying, and delivery of the milk, the chain becomes stronger. The child cries more, but the number of protothoughts also increases. However, the child cannot discriminate between the effectiveness of crying and "thinking."

Instead, within his reference, the thoughts have brought consequences: the milk. He does not realize that the crying was the actual factor. Slowly, the wishes and fantasies of early infancy are strengthened and rewarded. The child begins to think that his thoughts control the world around him. This sequence cannot be demonstrated easily in young infants since they do not talk. In order for them to relate their "thoughts," they must develop language. However, such conditioning can be clearly shown in adult speakers. There is little difference between the general learning patterns of infants and adults.

The impact of such "magical thinking" on the adult sensation of personal omnipotence is pervasive. By very simple extrapolation, the person begins to anticipate that his thoughts might control the universe. First, they control the presentation of food, then the parents, and finally the parent surrogate, God.

Later, in periods of helplessness, when all other forms of logic fail, these earlier forms of thinking recur. As the person lies dying, or when life reaches that last-ditch stage of tolerance, magical thinking emerges again. In fact, the primary condition for this type of thinking to be "resurrected" is near-death situations. The main components of this responding would involve "image action" or the "elimination" of the near-death or crisis situations by thinking.

One example that illustrates the characteristics of what magical imagery or superstitious thinking might contain is the following case of an "out-of-body experience":

> Suddenly, I felt the impact of the automobile and found myself looking down on my body. There was total pain and I hated the place. I wanted to leave and suddenly I was not there. I found that when I thought, I moved. So I thought about my home, and suddenly I was there walking into the front room and seeing my Mom cleaning the floor. I wondered where Dad was and then I was in another place, a strange place, where he was working. I felt panic for a moment and then a calm came over me and I saw the softest eyes that I have ever seen—a voice said "be still" and I knew it had been Christ.

In this experience, the primary control of the "scenes" was interpreted as "due to thinking." The person just thought about something and it appeared. (Considering the erroneous presumption that ideas are nonphysical, it is not surprising that "thinking" and "spirit" concepts are often fused.)

The consequences of magical thinking become extensions of the egocentric reference. Because of the sequence: thoughts, overt acts, and the resulting rewards (or punishments), accidental thoughts are maintained. This is a powerful superstitious behavior that is almost impossible to control.

To expose it for the illusion that it is, one must perceive the do-loop, the Catch-22. In order to "experience" anything, some type of thought process must be involved. But in order to realize that thoughts have absolutely nothing to do with the delivery of reward, one must not have any thoughts. But without any thoughts, one cannot experience the fact that the experiences are not true. When your logic is a do-loop, you'll never know your thinking occurs in circles. It appears only as an infinite line.

The compulsion creeps through adulthood. The egocentric person feels that his or her thoughts are also special. These people carefully guard a "new idea" as if it was some unique thing. The possibility that someone else may have thought about it before does not impress them. The fact that "the idea" is only a combination of words does not affect them.

Many people "just know" their thoughts or hunches may control the results of a lottery or the fall of dice. Each time the dice roll or the wheels turn and nothing happens, the hunches are forgotten or suppressed.

Then by chance alone (and nothing else), one single person wins (someone has to), and the hunches or other irrelevant ideas that preceded the win are reinforced. The winner "knew" he would win the prize. After all, a combination of the cousin's birthday and Uncle Bill's anniversary were used. Others hear, and secretly feel, "I am the next in line."

The ludicrous nature of this type of magical thinking is most apparent in the God Experience. Ultimately, as the final source of proof, the person relies on personal experience (his or her thoughts) to defend the validity of the event. In one form or another, the person contends that God has interacted with his or her *thoughts*. Yet, there is no real physical evidence.

Like the child who feels her wishes control and interact with the parents' behaviors, the convinced adult concludes that her thoughts interact with God. Somehow in the vast unknowns of time and space, God acts through the trivial nuances of human thinking. The absolute stupidity of the compulsion is not seen. Compelled by the conviction that one's thoughts are special and unique, the person assumes that something defined to include all time and space can be obtained by a few random fluctuations from a handful of neurons.

A sense of magic surplants the statistics of numbers. Each person believes that if the city is obliterated by an atomic blast, that he or she will (because of some special powers) survive. If the plane crashes, "I" will, by virtue of this unique condition, float to the ground. If everyone else dies of lung cancer from too many packs of cigarettes, "I" will not. There are always a few flukes in nature to reinforce that presumption.

Organized religions stroke this conviction and tell you what you want to hear (Clark 1958). You are told that you are unique and that God interacts through your personal experience. Clever con men also use this technique every time they portray the illusion of democracy by asking *you* to judge from personal experience. They, like religious leaders, know that few people will indict themselves by questioning their own experience.

We don't see the egocentric reference in ourselves. It is more easily seen when amplified and expanded to explain the universe. Whereas most of us display these symptoms only in times of personal crisis and alarm, this illusion runs rampant among the psychotic population. It is here that the egocentric reference is seen for what it is.

When the exaggeration of the normal egocentric reference occurs, thoughts appear to control the universe. People appear to directly interact with the patient's thinking or to control their behavior from a distance. References to telepathy and thought control are widespread.

For example, one middle-aged male, who was diagnosed as schizophrenic, reported:

> I am God. I know this since my thoughts control other people. I know my thoughts are responsible for the assassinations of the world. JFK and I are one. Since I have these thoughts, like the President and the Pope, and then the nations respond, there is no other possibility.

When confronted with the option that the events came *first* and the thoughts came afterward, the conviction of the egocentric reference prevailed. He merely smiled and said, "It is Christian to be persecuted."

The psychotic patient achieves the supreme form of egocentric reference. He reports thoughts that appear to control the universe. Unlike the philosopher who can examine universal questions of "the beginning" or "the end" and maintain the limitation, the psychotic thinker confuses the thin boundary between himself and the universe. The two, to him, are one.

It is not surprising when patient A-1405-1971 states that he could not move for two weeks, because if he did the world would be destroyed. When the egocentric reference predominates, the logic "my girlfriend is pregnant; I have never slept with her; hence I must be God" seems to make sense. The endless stream of Christs and self-styled sons of gods who have filled our mental institutions are only the extreme forms from our species' deep potential. They are the social embarrassments who we dare not consider.

You might simply say, "These are crazy people; they are not like us at all." You might be amused by the patient who assumed that he was being followed across Europe by Carlo Ponti, who was making film after film about the patient's life. You might smirk and look away when the patient insists that God is buried, like a honeycomb, within his brain.

It's always funnier when we talk about the other guy. But his thoughts are just as human as yours. His delusions are just as real as yours. If other people's thoughts are prone to the vagaries of biological artifacts and chemical disruptions, why should your ideas be any different? Why should your God Experience be any more than another perturbation within the cells of a human brain?

5
Memory Changes and the Maintenance of Contradictions

The consistency of the egocentric reference must be maintained. If there are clear contrivances and contradictions, even the most rabid believer would, sooner or later, see the discrepancies. A continued failure to realize experiential oddities can be traced to a property of human memory.

Memory is the ultimate measurement procedure of human experience. When we look out the window and see a stranger passing by, the information is processed quickly through the brain. Specific details of the perception are compared and referenced to similar situations of the past.

Is the stranger a friend? Do I know him? Is it a familiar face? Is he a potential threat to my existence? By using the memories of things that have already happened, quick and (for the most part) accurate answers can be gained.

Memory is the basis of the idiosyncratic properties of people that make them individuals. A person is identified by how he behaves in a certain context. Does he take draft beer or prefer a bottle? A person is defined by the details he remembers; does he recall attending first grade and knowing a little girl with pigtails?

In essence, the memories of a person define the self. Each person is the composite of those past events stored or correlated within brain space. Without them, there would be no past and without a past there would be nothing to compare to the present. We would live, like the young infant, in an eternal present.

Considering the importance of memory for the evaluation of contemporary experience, one would assume, almost reflexively, that memory is truly stable. Isn't what one remembers about long ago a ''mental picure'' of exactly how it was? Isn't memory like a photographic plate, on which the details of the past are fixed forever? The answer, quite emphatically, is no.

Memory is *not* fixed (Stern 1985). It can be modified by experiences after the event. Details of memories can be altered by the words and phrases used to code and to recall them. It happens to all of us, no matter how dumb, smart, or educated.

A famous scientist once said he remembered walking past a graveyard on the way to grade school. He even concluded that his preoccupation with death-related topics was tied to this early "trauma." But there never was any graveyard along the path to school. There was, however, a big, black dog that, to use a metaphor, almost "scared the child to death."

Emotional memories are prone to modification, especially when they tend to indict the concept of the self. After you have acted like an ass in public, you remember only the clever things you said. When recalling the time you acted like a brat and screamed because someone did not share your beliefs, you might recall it as a test. You say you knew what you were doing, that you were only testing people.

Sometimes memory is a completely unreliable measure of "experience." When certain parts of the human brain are stimulated abnormally, memory is affected. Details of perceptions can be lost, sequences of events can be changed, and fantasies can be substituted for reality. Once the memory is stored, the modifications will appear as real as any other. It will be recalled as a clear and true event that actually happened. No amount of regression hypnosis or other measures of "the truth" will alter the conviction.

One clinical psychologist (who wished to remain anonymous), whose religious beliefs can be traced to a single event in childhood, recalls:

> I clearly remember my first experience with our Creator—if you want to call Him the Infinite Force of the Eternal Consciousness, that's fine with me. Anyway, he appeared to me while I was a young child, late one night when I was in bed. I know I wasn't asleep—I could certainly tell the difference. He told me that he was touching me through an angel. I remember that so vividly, even now when I think of it, especially late at night, I feel shivers run down my spine. It was very real and absolutely nothing like the psychiatric types we see every day.

When asked if he had been sick or had been ill during that period, the psychologist laughed and stated, "I'm trained in clinical techniques—don't you think I could tell the difference between a fever delirium and a veridical event? Besides, I have experienced God many times since then, even if the first time had been a case of simple hallucination."

The same psychologist's parents remember the episode well. Indeed, he had been sick with scarlet fever and had repeatedly referred to the presence of "things" within his room. During this period, the young man displayed severe hyperthermia and the children's aspirin they gave him did not work effectively. (There is a high probability that he may have seizured.) The parents remember the episode clearly, because the child kept referring to being "visited by an angel just like Samuel'' and of ''hearing his name called.'' The story had been told to the young man during one of his first exposures to a church setting, the previous week.

The parents had not mentioned the episode to the psychologist; in fact, they concluded it was quite trivial. When queried directly, they thought he had forgotten about the experience completely (they suspected it has been a type of night terror). Only much later were they surprised that the child had some memory, although a different one, of the episode. They had decided that since the young man felt so strongly about the experience, it was not their role to destroy his faith.

Transient dysfunction of the parts of the brain so intimately involved with remembering can produce some pretty unusual experiences. During these periods, your name may be ''called'' while you are standing in a group of people. A blob of light may be seen as you look out of a ten-story building in downtown New York City, or a small humanoid may stop you on the way home from work to tell you, ''You're going to hurt your arm if you do not repent.''

As long as memory is used as the reference, there is absolutely no way the person could recognize errors. Changes in memory, due to chemical flukes of long-term shortage or to electrical transients during the acquisition, will not be realized since the memory is being used to measure memory.

Over time, these ''experiences'' are modified to fit into the context of things. Their strangeness and oddity are removed and the personal significance is enhanced. It was no longer a voice in the midst of a crowd of people, but a personal proof of the spirit. It was no longer a blob of light but an angel who cured you of cancer. It was no longer an odd being with a trivial piece of data but a galactic messenger with cosmic tidings.

Within this floating baseline exists a world of apparent stability. No wonder the believers and the embracers of the God Experience are obsessed with the proof of personal experience. Their private lives, their definition of self, rely on the ability to believe in the infallibility of their own egocentric expressions.

No doubt most discrepancies could be detected if comparisons were made with written records, photographs, or other people's memories. But a few convictions, like the God Experience, depend on the existence of the egocentric experience itself. Other people's reports appear only as verifications. They, too, are contaminated by the same illusions.

However, the world is full of constant challenges about the truth of those experiences. People like you, who also believe they are special, die in automobile accidents. People like you, who have experienced God in a personal way, show the same distributions of diseases. Religious adherents die of heart attacks and bursting arteries in the brain just like nonbelievers.

How can people acknowledge the limits of the human body on one hand, and on the other maintain that the spirit is immortal? How can people insist on seeing the facts in everyday life and then have the faith of children when listening to the Bible, the Koran, and other scriptures of the past?

The process involved must be a persistent human behavior, for there are endless examples in our daily lives. We are taught to abhor killing, but we adore and imitate the generals who have killed millions. We are taught that living in peace is the highest form of human existence. Yet in history books, the kings who lived in peace attract little notice. The reigns that were characterized by wars and bloodshed are the subject of volumes.

We learn that all men are created equal, but then we flee the cities when minorities move in beside us. We are taught to turn the other cheek as a sign of Christian understanding, but we scorn the person who turns aside instead of fighting, and call him coward. We may tell him he was right and then shun him. The same educated men who insist that women should have an equal opportunity in the marketplace make sure their wives stay home to tend the kitchen and raise the kids.

Contradictory and logically inconsistent learned behavior is not a sign, necessarily, of neurosis. Because of the nature of human learning, there are many normal instances where we learn one set of behaviors in one situation and a completely different (and sometimes contradictory) set of behaviors in another (Houstan 1986). The process by which clusters of behaviors are kept separate can be called *compartmentalization*.

A long as contradictory responses are not displayed in the same place and at the same time, the discrepancies will not be apparent. When two sets of antagonistic responses are displayed, such as "in order to capture a village you must destroy it first," anxiety frequently follows.

Obviously, the simplest way to avoid the anxiety of conflict is to prevent the sequential or simultaneous display of incompatible responses. It may involve simple avoidance of the two situations or even some clever rationalization, such as, "No one else is really as unique as I am."

When applied to thinking, compartmentalization means learning to keep antagonistic or anxiety-provoking thoughts apart. This separation can also be accomplished by simply avoiding the stimuli that will evoke the conflict. The person may avoid reading certain books, or in more severe instances, actually burn them.

Some clusters of thoughts are avoided totally. The person cannot "remember" the material at all, although the effects of the learning still influence overt behavior. This type of avoidance is called *suppression* or *repression*, depending on the severity. Anxiety is reduced at the cost of accurate recall.

In some cases, the person may have a complete amnesia of certain behaviors, except in the situations in which they were learned. This kind of context-dependent learning will be discussed again in Chapter 6. Memories of these "other" behaviors can be stimulated, often with the shock of sudden recognition, when other people display similar patterns.

The effects of compartmentalization can range from everyday fragments to changes in the entire personality. For example, in school or at church, you may answer with conviction that one creed is just different but not better from another. The next day, when you are sitting around the bar talking with friends, you may laugh at a joke about the inferiority of niggers, honkies, or jews. The discrepancy is not obvious; the two behaviors have been learned in different places.

Another example is the pious hypocrite. These individuals are usually ardent churchgoers. On Sunday, they sit in the pews and nod with the words of the sermon. They agree that drinking is wrong, smoking is bad, and coveting other men's wives is sinful. In fact, they may actually believe it, on Sunday. However, for the rest of the week, these individuals may drink excessively, beat their children, cheat on their wives, and engage in general "sinful" behaviors. When asked if they are churchgoers, they gladly acknowledge the fact. The discrepancy is not seen. A hypocrite may not always recognize his own reflection.

The patchwork of behaviors we call our personality becomes more obvious (but more difficult to detect) when time becomes a variable. New habits are built on old ones, often in random and inconsistent ways. There is no necessary logic to the process. Upon the young bigot is built the egalitarian, each with its own trigger and place to be displayed.

The compartmentalization of learning is a difficult barrier to break. Even with the knowledge of modern behavioral science and the proficiency of teaching techniques, old habits die hard. I have spent weeks explaining the dangers of calling children "idiots" and "morons." Reams and reams of data are presented to demonstrate the deleterious effects these labels have on the child's self-concept.

The parents sit there, night after night, shaking their heads in disbelief at how other people could be so mean to their kids. They would never do such a thing. Then they leave the university and return to their homes where they beat their kids, call them names, and invoke their own selfish wishes as universal standards.

Compartmentalization can also be seen in the way one approaches problems. Perhaps the most apt example of compartmentalization of thinking can be found in the religious scientist. Even the term, technically speaking, is contradictory. Religious scientists are usually trained in the natural sciences, such as physics, chemistry, or biology. Typically, they have little empirical experience of behavioral principles or in the objective evaluation of human behavior. Instead, they depend on their own experiences or Biblical opinions in order to explain human activity.

This type is the Jekyll and Hyde of academia. Dressed in lab coats and other symbols of status, these people insist on the use of critical thinking. During the day, they talk about data, the problems of measurement, and the importance of knowing the limitations of analytical procedures. They display in the laboratories the behavior they have learned in that context. They worship "pure reason" and the consistencies in data. They extrapolate from established principles and are suspicious of shady hypotheses, weak theories, and speculations that have no data base. Then these scientists leave the laboratory behind, get into their cars, and go home for the weekend. There, they make statements like, "Blood is thicker than water," or "There are some things that people should not investigate." On Sundays, they go to church and kneel at the altar of impulse, hearsay, and faith.

In an objective perspective and placed within the comprehension of a single paragraph, the discrepancies would be evident even to these people. However, since the intervals of time are so long, juxtaposition and confrontation rarely occur. Instead, they continue to live in a world in which lip service to data exists side by side with the most childish forms of thinking.

Are these people nuts? No, they are normal. Even though, as scientists, they are suppose to exemplify the extreme opposite to a reliance on personal experience, they are still human. They fear their personal extinction and are still prone to occasional cosmic highs.

The sciences are methods, not people. One must not confuse the two. Scientific behavior is described and defined according to the techniques employed and the measurements taken. It is characterized by the logic of the interpretation and the methods by which the conclusions are obtained. Human beings are *not* inherently scientists; every so often, they just happen to display scientific behavior.

There are many predictable solutions to the latent conflict between daily rationality and nightly belief. The most primitive solution is to deny any discrepancy at all. Such individuals simply state there is no difference between the limits of personal experiences and those of scientific experimentation. They usually don't last very long. The insulation is too thin.

A second solution is to insist that personal experience and objective events exist in two separate universes. Scientists, for example, contend with this solution that the physical universe is ruled by one set of principles while the mental world is ruled by another. Then there is the spiritual world, an odd bastard of the latter, that has no principles at all.

To hold this idea, the person must maintain an ignorance of human behavior. A person whose life is based on this assumption must never realize that there is little difference between "mental" life and other physical processes. If the similarity was known, the anxiety would become incapacitating. There would be absolutely no difference between the statistical variations of an inert piece of matter and the existence of the self.

To fulfill this belief, any suggestion that mental or private experience is *not* beyond the limits of physical principles must be eliminated. Such logic requires the constant invalidation of behavioral analyses. Psychology, sociology, or any of the social sciences must be constantly shown as ineffective, trivial, and inconsistent.

The scheme is not always successful. As human behavior becomes more predictable, the idea of a mental universe begins to shatter. Then, slowly, scientific measurement begins to erode the last fortress of the egocentric reference: the "spirit."

Complex arguments are not trustworthy. Someday, they could be solved. A simpler way is to define the discrepancy away. "All right," the religious scientist thinks, "I'll concede that the behaviors of the planets, chairs, and toads are based on physical principles. However, the existence of the spirit is totally beyond all that."

It is a comfortable default, a palatable escape to the inevitable challenge to the petty nature of personal experience. By simply defining the problem away, the imminent anxiety is removed. With a wave of the hand, the problem seems to go away.

But it never really goes away. There are always gnawing inconsistencies. If there are physical, mental, and spiritual things, why are there gaping contradictions only in the latter? A rock falls at 32 feet per second, no matter what one's religious preference. Human beings satiate to novelties as a function of the number of uses per unit time and the duration of each use. But believers in God, Allah, and Buddah are all convinced of completely different versions of the world.

Next, there is the problem of being sure the spiritual existence is really there. When psychotics in a ward are convinced of their God Experience and the basic themes do not vary from his own, how does the religious scientist tell the difference? He can invoke excuses and rationalizations. These people are different because they are possessed by demons, devils, or some bad thing. Or, the religious scientist could pretend a quasineural sophistication. He could argue that the spirit is mediated through the brain. When certain portions of the brain dysfunction, an excess of God Experiences are displayed.

But if the spirit is mediated through brain cells, how does one know it's there? If drugs, electrical disorders, general deterioration, or chemical peculiarities can induce identical experiences, how can one tell when the *real* spirit has been the cause? How does one know for sure? Because a pile of old pages says so?

And so, slowly, the compartmentalization begins to break down and the two incompatible worlds of hard data and personal experience come together. The anxiety begins. It is subtle, at first, a creeping unlabelled thing that is at the tip of the tongue. Sometimes he wakes in the middle of the night for no apparent reason. He finds himself avoiding talks about death and missing routine funerals. The thought of nuclear annihilation and complete disintegration scares him to the core. Would the "I" survive the heat of that holocaust?

So the religious scientist begins to search for proofs for the survival of his personal experience. He thirsts for anecdotal cases of "people who have returned from the grave" and of true mystical experiences (Smith 1954). But then he sees the wards full of mental patients who live in a world of gods and devils and feelings of personal omnipotence. He watches old people, no matter how clever they *once* were, grasping at every proof of an afterlife.

As religious assumptions are set side by side with the objectivity of scientific analyses, faith begins to wane. As science explains and limits ancient mysteries, the uniqueness of personal conviction is threatened. When the separation of the Red Sea can be explained in terms of seismic tidal waves and the holy behavior of King Saul becomes nothing more than a mundane case of manic depression, the line becomes very thin.

The house of cards begins to fall. The miracle of Elijah throwing meal into the porridge becomes a single exercise in killing spores. Lazarus was no longer a dead man but a cataleptic person who reflected the perennial fear of being buried alive. Moses merely struck some stones, already damp with moisture, and released an underground stream that had eroded into the outcrop.

Christ did no walk *on* the water but *by* the water because the same preposition in Greek can refer to either. It's a matter of context. Christ was not a special person but probably a harmless psychotic (since we do not have norms for that period, we cannot be sure) who was prone to speaking in riddles and occasional emotional outbursts. Like many hundreds of would-be messiahs, each with their own charisma (who arose in response to Roman rule), Christ would have died in obscurity had it not been for the business sense of Paul.

And finally, Jehovah is seen for what he was, a reflection of the contemporary human behavior. He is reduced to little more than a limbic animal with frontal lobe damage who was prone to indiscriminate rage and ruthless impulse. He was ignorant of basic learning principles and inconsistently punished his people. Like the repressed human emotions from which he was created, Jehovah was nothing more than a primitive hodge-podge of magical thinking and irrationality.

To prevent logic from ravaging the sacred past, a simple solution appears to the person faced with this crisis: restrict the discussion and make the topic taboo. An old theme appears once again. Everything is amenable to analysis *except*. . . . Compartmentalization occurs and the anxiety lessens. The world seems right once more.

One can appreciate the dilemma of the religious scientist or the educated believer. To maintain his or her personal integration, more and more exceptions must be made. In the end, the belief becomes ludicrous. The person stops thinking about the problem altogether and simply tells you, "It is a private thing" or that he or she is "deeply religious." With this evasion, people leave him or her alone. With this solution, he or she can survive.

Education and the scientific understanding of human behavior are a constant threat to the process of compartmentalization. As long as people remain ignorant, the world can be seen in the simple-minded trichotomies of physical, mental, and spiritual. Daily contradictions can abound.

Religious organizations encourage compartmentalized behaviors. "Give unto Caesar that which is Caesar's and give unto God that which is God's" is just one of the many statements that attempt to justify such segregation of beliefs. It says display one set of behaviors in one situation and another set of behaviors, even if they are contradictory, in another.

God Experiences foster this duality as well. How can the person conclude any differently? When the brain, the ultimate tool of measurement in this infinite space, is stimulated, how can the reality of the experience be challenged? There is simply "me" and then there is everyone else. I am an exception to the rule.

Is it any wonder then that people who score highest on religious scales are also those who are prone to the greatest bigotry? Is it any wonder that in order to save the souls of "the primitives," missionaries beat and starved hundreds of cultures for their own good? Is it any wonder that brilliant men make bombs that can wipe us all from the surface of the earth and still privately believe that their souls will live forever? Is it any wonder that millions of people hold Bibles in one hand and guns in the other?

6
The Expectation of God: Conditioning and Sources of the Details

The expectation of a god or a supreme being and the details of such a concept are due primarily to the early social patterns of the human primate. We are not suddenly born as individuals, capable of locomotion and self-control. Instead, we spend years and sometimes decades as a total function of other people. These people include our parents, teachers, and other symbols of the social order.

For the first two years of life, the human being is a passive organism, at the mercy of the people around him or her. He or she cannot obtain his or her own food, warmth, or bodily comfort. Instead, he or she must find these essential life elements by manipulating the environment.

These manipulations are rewarded by their consequences. The child learns that a cry is followed by the delivery of milk, the mother's warmth, or the removal of an uncomfortable diaper. After thousands of cries and the consequent responses of the parents (or their substitutes), the child begins to anticipate that someone or something will come. The expectancy is as natural as human behavior.

The young infant or child learns that helplessness can be eliminated or reduced by crying out. A simple cry or related vocalization brings warmth, food, and most of all, security. When the parents are near, the universe is complete. The only anxiety is the anticipation of their removal; this, too, is learned.

Within the infant's logic, the parents have all the characteristics of the adult concept of God. To the young infant, whose quasi-experiences are a confusing blend of faces and feelings, the parents are everywhere. To the young infant, whose sense of time is like an eternal present, the parents live forever. They are indeed omnipotent.

Slowly, the child learns that she can act upon the environment by herself.

She learns that if the hand is moved, the pacifier can be placed in the mouth. If the legs are moved, the shining trinket on the table can be taken. If the cup is grasped, the milk can be enjoyed. All of these things can take place, without the parents' help.

Occasionally, the world does not seem to go very well for the young tot. No matter what ingenuity she can muster, the problem cannot be solved. The situation is hopeless. But then she cries and the mother or father appears and solves the problem for her. Once again, the feeling of *helplessness* has been removed by calling out.

In this instance, the child has demonstrated one of the most frequent behaviors in human experience: *context-dependent learning* (Houstan 1986). Stated simply, it means that behavior learned in certain conditions, near certain places or people or during specific times, will be more likely to occur when those situations are repeated.

Behaviors derived from context-dependent learning are the major components of our personality. How often have you experienced the following example? Just before leaving for work in the morning, you are asked (or told) to buy a loaf of bread or a quart of milk. You leave the house for work and completely forget the request. That night, as you turn into the driveway or start to walk up the stairs to the apartment, the request is suddenly remembered. You slap your head (or swear) and say, "How could I forget?"

In this instance, the context is the home or house. The memory of the request to buy the bread or milk has been associated with that cue. When the cue is not visible, the memory is not recalled. Stated in a more popular fashion, it is an example of "out of sight, out of mind."

If memories are dependent on the context within which they were learned, then the best recall should occur in the original place of learning. This statement is certainly true. When you want to remember the details of youth, return to the homestead or to the old hangout. As you walk into the patterns of yesterday, an odd sense of familiarity creeps through your body.

As you pick up childhood objects or see old buildings, vivid images from the past return. Things you have not thought about for years, memories that you are surprised even to recall, are suddenly available for inspection. Missing pieces fall into place and for a brief moment you are suspended in reminiscence.

However, a condition, place, or time does *not* have to be *exactly* like the original in order to evoke learned memories. This capacity is called the property of *stimulus generalization* (Hergenhahn 1982). It simply states that the more similar a situation is to a previous one, the more likely the thoughts and memories paired with the old situation will be rememberd in the new one.

This property is responsible for most of our "first impressions" or gut attractions and repulsions. You may not like a woman because she reminds you of Aunt Martha. The term "remind" is simply another way of saying "stimulus generalization." Most people are unaware of the specific characteristics that the new person shares with people from the past.

Stimulus generalization is most evident when adults attend university (for the first time) to continue their education. Even though they are now 30 or 40 years old, they display the behaviors last associated with learning: those of high school. Much to the surprise of their family (and later to themselves), they laugh and giggle and feel the emotions of youth. For a brief time, they may actually forget about the family and spouses at home.

Responses can also be associated with the *behavioral patterns* of other people. If you have learned to fear your father, because he beat you inconsistently, then certain behaviors displayed by the father may evoke experiences of anxiety or anticipation of punishment. The same experiences may generalize to other men such as army sergeants, police officers, judges, or professors who happen to act in a very similar manner.

The extent to which you will generalize your uneasiness to the presence of other people depends on emotional arousal. If you are emotionally upset, unsure of who you are, or scared, the stimulus generalization widens. You may even fear people who show just *one* of the basic behaviors of the father.

Thoughts or responses may also be tied to certain *bodily conditions*. For example, the song you heard when you first woke up in the morning usually "pops into mind" when you are about to fall asleep at night. In this instance, the two bodily conditions, waking up and falling asleep, are very similar. During the day, when the bodily conditions were quite different, the song was not recalled at all!

Long-term state-dependent memories occur during illness. During periods when you are weak with the flu and drifting in and out of consciousness, memories of events that occurred during *other periods* of sickness are vividly recalled. Suddenly you can remember all the times you felt this way as a child, as an adolescent, or as an adult. The specific events—the smells of medicine and mustard plasters, the taste of ice cream and ginger ale—suddenly burst into awareness.

When you are not sick, these old memories are not recalled. But they are not lost, they are just not remembered. They can be carried for years, even a lifetime, with the same crisp, emotional details that comprised the first experience.

Not surprisingly, during periods of helplessness, memories and thoughts are evoked that were initially learned in those situations. When your boyfriend leaves or your wife dies, who do you call? When you have tried a problem again and again and there is no answer, for whom do you ask? In most cases, especially for the young, the answer is the parents. Sometimes, using the principle of stimulus generalization, a substitute like an older friend, or minister or priest is called.

In extreme cases, adults may call for their mother or father. As people lay slowly dying, helpless and immobile like the infantile condition, the demands for their mother or father are often heard. These cries are not heard if the death is sudden or one of surprise. Since the context is different, other behaviors, typically vocalizations of awe or curses are used.

The *anticipation* that *someone* will come is unaltered as the person lies immobile and helpless. However, the details have been changed by learning. The adult has been shaped by years of rewards and punishments. He has learned complex symbols and combinations of powerful words. The infantile absolutes of everywhere and everything are still expected, but the particulars have changed.

The parents no longer have the properties of omnipotence and omnipresence. Through experience, the adult has learned that parents are discrete and mortal beings with limited space and little time. The childhood expectations have been generalized to God.

But how is this generalization done? It is so simple and so common that we do not see the process because of its persistence. The quality of parental omnipotence is passed on to God expectations by the language of association.

The principle of association is the cornerstone of personality. It states that two events, objects, or things occurring together in space and time will be associated. This means that when one of the objects or events is presented, the other will be recalled.

This is the essence of language learning. Initially when the infant is presented with a bottle, the mother uses the word "bottle." After several pairings of the word and the object, the child begins to say the word "bottle" or some close approximation. When the older child is asked to describe what a bottle is (without the object), the details reflect the experiences he has had with bottles.

In this way, the properties of objects are transferred to words. Later, when the child grows older, the meaning of the old words can be transferred to new or unknown cues in a similar manner. The simplest examples of a transfer are definitions and descriptions with the format "———is———." Specific examples are "Jim is bad" or "The dog is an animal."

The importance of association starts at the beginning of the child's life. Initially, the child responds to the biological demands of food, warmth, touch, and the elimination of wastes. These requirements are innate—they are biological properties of the child.

The color of the mother's hair, the patterns of her face, or her smells are not important then. Only after the repeated presentation of these particular characteristics of the mother are paired with the essential biological requirements, does the mother as a person achieve any value for the child.

Once learned, these features become important. Whereas the child would have responded initially to any lactating female, he now responds optimally to the female to which he has been exposed most. Her particular smells, touch, and looks unleash all of the security and pleasures initially produced by biological stimuli. There are also other sensations, like those of trust and security.

Slowly and subtly, the powerful gut associations and expectations elicited by the mother or mother surrogate are translated into words. One of the first words to be heard by a child in the English language is "love." The mother frequently says, in various forms: "I love you." "Love," initially an unintelligible sound, becomes paired with the mother's presence; it develops a meaning.

The powerful associations of the word "love" can be easily passed on to things that cannot be seen or proven. By using the simple sentence, "God is love," all of the associations paired with love can be transferred to God. The word "God" becomes associated with the security and the quiescence of those early parental relationships (Persinger 1985).

The associations with God do not end there. Parental protection does not help the person to live forever. To obtain this property, the concept of God (no matter what the culture) is ultimately associated with the adult sense of infinite time and space. It is perfused with the infantile experience of eternity and omnipotence.

Details of the God Concept are determined by the specific experience of the person. To be consistent with the present argument, people from different cultures (that is, different shared experiences) should report different depictions of God. This prediction is supported by cross-cultural evidence from anthropological studies. The general characteristics of different gods from different cultures reflect the rituals and learning patterns of the people.

Most of all, the details of God reflect the early learning of the people within the culture. Matrilineal cultures (societies whose kinship lines are traced through the mother's family and not the father's predecessors) have female gods. In patrilineal cultures, where the male line is most important, the god is portrayed with clear masculine features.

When the child-rearing practices of a society are severe, the negative properties are projected onto the concept of God. The local deity is depicted as punishing and aversive; it is a thing that must be appeased by pain or sacrifice. In short, God must be placated and left alone, least he punish the person with death and damnation.

Appeals to such gods during periods of helplessness are less likely. They do occur when all else fails, since the person had, as a child, some experience of expectation. If the parents had not responded to his early cries, he would not have survived. The child must be given food and care in order to survive. With these presentations, the expectation that *someone* will come during helplessness is shaped and rewarded.

Cultures that display more severe childhood rearing practices, such as early weaning, frequent punishment for crying, and early failure to attend to the child's needs, worship gods that show this propensity. They are fickle beings who, at a whim, withdraw the option for eternity. The children of these cultures do not understand why the sudden changes in status occur; the people in these cultures cannot understand why God wreaks havoc one day and nurtures them the next.

On the other hand, cultures with less severe child-rearing practices cast God in different roles. Longer periods of intimate contact between the child and mother allow stronger conditioning of expectations. The child has a longer learning history of crying and receiving milk, whimpering and receiving attention, cuddling and receiving warmth. Weaning is completed gradually, so that the child can learn other options.

Gods of cultures whose members practice positive child-rearing behaviors are also friendly and positive. The person experiences them in a one-to-one relationship. God is a comfortable thing with whom the person can share a close communion. It is warm and always there; the sense of security can be found anywhere, anytime.

The God Concept in modern Western culture is also determined by the associations and experiences of the first few years of life. God is seen, not surprisingly, as the Father (and not the Mother). Christian followers reinforce this concept by such rituals as the Lord's Prayer ("Our Father, who art in heaven. . . . ").

References to God are filled with implications of a parental relationship. The believer is seen as "a child of God," or a member of "the flock," of which God is the shepherd. Although the descriptions and parables may change, the theme remains the same: God is the superparent.

When generalized to the God Concept, the childhood magic of the omnipotent and omniscient parent survives. The person can be safe and secure within the protection of the parent surrogate. Like the parent who meets the demands of the infant, God is always there when needed.

The essential theme of God as a helpful friend and source of security is more pronounced among children or adults who have not paired the normal associations to the word "father." God is seen functionally as a maternal figure around which people (children or adults) dance, sing, and have fun.

In fact, the Catholic concept of the Virgin Mary has acquired these properties. Like the relationship in many families where the mother must intercede for the child with the husband, the Mother of God is key. Although the person acknowledges the supremacy of the male-like God, the Mother image is the one associated with actual intimacy, happiness, and security.

Pairing of the word *father* with the God Concept (as in the Lord's Prayer) transfers many of the associations of father to the God image. In contemporary Western culture, the father is (in general) associated with the source of rewards and ultimate punishments. The father may be friendly, but he is also the one who punishes the transgressor.

The father as a source of ambivalence is a persistent theme in the family structure; it reappears in the concept of God. He is usually seen as the source of reward (eternal survival, or in cruder times; simple riches) and of punishment (damnation, eternal torment, or personal failure).

Like the typical human father, this God Concept must be feared. If the believer deviates from the dictates of the "rules" of God, then punishment follows. The stakes are much higher, however. The believer does not lose her car privileges or the weekly allowance. Instead, she loses her soul.

Anticipation of punishment for breaking the rules induces anxiety. Anxiety, in milder forms, is a potent modifier of behavior. The mere anticipation of breaking a rule results in the apprehension of punishment. This apprehension is only removed when the believer no longer thinks about committing the transgression.

The importance of this kind of behavioral control over the integrity of a society can be seen. Since anxiety is much worse than the actual punishment (and this has been shown time and time again in psychology laboratories), the threat of punishment can be used to check deviations and manipulate behavior. People rarely commit offenses against God because of the anticipation of punishment, the dissolution of the self and eternal pain.

Those who do defy God have had behavioral histories of obtaining parental or group attention by rebellion or antagonism. Their behavior has been maintained by the criticisms of society. Since deviations from the "rules" generate this type of critical attention, these heretics and spiritual criminals continue to challenge the assumptions.

People from cultures that maintain a more strict description of the father's role in reward and punishment have gods that reflect these associations. God is seen as an absolute authority whose dictates must never be challenged. The believer is not asked to attend a spiritual gathering or to love the deity; he is told to obey. Like the biological father whose basic logic is, "This is so because I say it is," there is no logic or rationality to the dictates of God.

The normal behaviors of human existence are paralleled in the way people respond to God. Deviations from the rules the person has learned result in an anticipation of punishment. This anticipation of punishment precipitates anxiety and guilt. The anxiety and guilt can be so intense that the child is compelled to confess.

Confession has an important consequence: it relieves anxiety. After the child tells the parent how he has deviated from the rules, the anticipation of punishment is relieved. Psychologists describe this procedure in a number of ways, such as "cognitive dissonance" or the "discrepancy between what is expected and what is done." Regardless of the name, the effects are the same—psychological stability is regained.

The importance of learning in the experience of anxiety and guilt is clearly seen within our culture. One is amazed at the *arbitrary* classes of events that make some people feel guilty and others feel good. Some people have multiple sexual relationships and feel no qualms; others, no matter how much they rationalize, always feel somewhat dirty and a little ashamed. The critical feature is not the act, but the rewards and punishments that have been paired with certain behaviors.

The rules of God are called "morals," "commandments," or "dictates."

When the believer breaks these rules, the anticipation of punishment also unleashes the devastation of anxiety and guilt. Although the intensity of the anxiety will vary with how severely these rules have been punished and rewarded, some psychological incapacitation will occur.

During these periods, the person experiences foreboding and fear. He feels cheap, diminutive and not fit to live; he hates himself. The anticipation can be so intense that major behavioral patterns of personality are suppressed. When this happens, the person cannot cope with even the simplest daily crisis. This is called a "nervous breakdown."

It is not surprising that the major method for alleviating this anxiety is confession to the abstract from which it originates, or God. During these periods of confession, the person tells all to God (or his representatives). The consequent sense of a "burden removed" (much like the experience of telling the parent that you have stolen the cookie from the forbidden jar) results in an exhilaration that parallels the euphoria of mania.

One case history that demonstrates this typical behavior projected onto the God concept involves a 24-year-old woman. She had been reared in a strict family where complete submission to the dominant male (in this case, the husband) was observed. The marriage had been arranged by the parents, and there were few emotional behaviors shared by the woman and her husband.

The woman was intelligent, an 'A' student and well organized. She could discriminate various fine points about human behavior; in some respects, she was self-actualized. For example, she was not disappointed when people deviated from her expectations. She was not shocked when told that a local priest was found to have impregnated a nun.

While at university, she became more and more dissatisfied with the dead-end and dull flavor of her life. She had an affair with another class member for whom she had the first adult feelings of her life. After about three months, she became pregnant, an event that was followed by the termination of the relationship. The sudden loss of her lover resulted in severe depression.

Shortly afterward, she was told that she had had a "nervous breakdown." She experienced several anxiety attacks and then told her husband about the pregnancy (something that would have been obvious before long). Since he was vasectomized, there were few alternative explanations. She was called an adulteress and spurned by her family.

After attempting suicide, she finally consulted a religious person. With his guidance, she spent several weeks praying and repenting. Suddenly one night, she felt God say to her, "You are forgiven." The experience was associated with a compulsion to spread the joy of God. She returned to her husband (inentally, after much intercedence by the religious person) and became a radical born-again Christian.

Two years after the conversion, she was still active in church work. She had lost interest in studying psychology, since "everything you wanted to know was in the Bible." Instead, she became interested in computer technology. To her, the world is seen as good or evil. No one can truly work except through the will of God. Anyone who deviates from the will of God is considered potentially dangerous or a topic for prayer.

Except for the involvement of God in the experience, the anxiety, personality deterioration, and restoration following anxiety reduction (in this case by confession and crying for help), are typical response sequences. However, when the adult self is involved and the breach of rules involves morality, the association with God is expected.

If the details of God are determined by the experience and learning of the person, then the concept should also vary with the age and education of the individual. The child sees God as a friendly parent, as a manlike spirit with a long beard. The adolescent sees God as a helpful parent who guides and gives advice, but who must never be challenged.

The adult's concept of God is much more variable. Although formal education (such as university or post-secondary training) is important, an equally critical factor is the amount of *personal differentiation*. A person who never really acted singly is still a child. These people still see themselves in the role of a child and God as a parent.

Such a concept is typical of people who have quickly moved from a home structure into marriage. They have never spent much time by themselves or challenged the limits of their personality. Usually they live in psychological straight jackets of *do*s and *don't*s. Deviations from the straight and narrow produce instant anxiety.

These people often have an impressive formal education. They may be scientists who contribute to such areas as biology, physics, or astronomy. Within a working context, these men and women can be witty, brilliant, and apparently objective.

At home, they crawl on their knees in prayer when things they wish for do not come true. The same people who celebrate human intelligence for solving problems beg for God's solutions. The same man that publicly supports equality of the sexes feels his wife's role is at home. Simple-minded psychology and Biblical word salad govern their lives.

People who have had more varied experiences view God in a less conventional manner. The physicist does not see God as a spirit who juggles the cosmos. He is seen as a force or unity or perfection that coordinates "the music of the spheres."

The mathematician does not see a man dressed in a robe surrounded by dancing children. Instead, she sees the spirit of the great final equation from which all is generated. The humanitarian, who has seen people starve to death, sees only absurdity in the belief they died because God willed it. To him, God is humanity and nothing more.

Although God may be seen in myriad ways, the theme is always one of helplessness. It occurs when the person can no longer solve the problems of psychological survival. The sense of helplessness can occur quickly or develop slowly with the maturation and development of the experiences each person calls "the self."

Acute helplessness occurs during periods of *unexpected*, imminent death, when the prospect of personal termination is suddenly acknowledged. There are three clear stages in this type of helplessness.

First, there is the rational, problem-solving stage of adult behavior. Various solutions are considered, tested, and rejected. If the person is about to drown because the car has suddenly run off the road into a deep, cold river, the decision may be made to swim. Various solutions are considered. He or she thinks, "First I will open the window, then I will pull myself outside the car, . . . then. . . . "

The second stage is the bull-dozing stage; it occurs when panic overcomes the discriminative inhibition of the frontal lobes. Precise ideas are no longer considered. The person flails and pushes. Even simple solutions are ignored. This type of mentality is typically displayed during fire panics when people push at a "pull door." Instead of simply stopping and pulling the door and saving their lives, the panic usually ends in disaster. After the fact, when people are more rational, they wonder how such a simple solution could have been overlooked. You have to be there.

The third stage is the experience of helplessness. As the person loses the strength to struggle, because of damaged tissue or lack of oxygen, fear gives way to a passive resignation. People who have been close to death report they felt like "accepting it." It is then, during the psychological condition of helplessness, that the God Experience typically occurs. No doubt, it may be a consequence of the biological conditions (of hypoxia or general tissue damage) that occur during acute conditions. However, the experience can also be predicted by understanding the psychological condition of helplessness.

Once this condition occurs, the person feels a sense of expectation that someone will come to the rescue and save the self. Typical experiences are images of dead relatives, usually parents or parent surrogates (such as aunts or uncles), who smile, wave, and approach the dying person. Since the situation is clearly death-dominant, all of the associations privately paired with that theme are evoked.

If the person has associated parent to God, God to heaven, and heaven to angels and pearly gates then the period of helplessness will elicit the experiences of angels smiling and the vision of heavenly gates. If the person has associated parents with God, God with heaven, and heaven with some magnificent garden within which people smile and dance around, then the dying person will be immersed within the scene.

Of course, the experience (in modern Western culture) will be attractive for two reasons. First, God is associated with very positive things. This is particularly true for believers. Second, anticipations of negative things, such as pain and torture, are not likely to occur. Events that are aversive and punished are not easily remembered, even in crisis situations.

The infant-like nature of the experience is seen by the heavy loading from the primitive perceptions of early childhood. In addition to the obvious parental behaviors of the images, there are smiles, laughter, and repeated references to food. The land of milk and honey is an appetizing expectation, especially if you've had a history of episodic starvation.

The magical nature of the experience of helplessness is also evident in the images. Many people feel that they are really not going to die, but transcend the situation. Mountain climbers who have fallen but were caught by safety ropes say they felt like they could "fly and stop falling" or "just think their way onto the limb of a nearby tree."

Helplessness can occur in less dramatic conditions. Any kind of severe psychological helplessness can elicit God Experiences. Common precipitating factors are: rejection by a girlfriend or a boyfriend, loss of a job, leaving home (to attend a university, college), and retirement.

The degree of helplessness and the likelihood of a God Experience are directly related to how much the concept of self has been tied to the conditions that have been changed. If the person has defined her life and herself "as an aerospace engineer," the sudden loss of a job could be catastrophic. A person who only sees work as a job but has defined himself as a family man or a jack-of-all-trades, would be less adversely affected by the impact.

One minister was "called by God" during a peak of helplessness. He had been rejected by his girlfriend and felt lost. He started to cry and then heard God speak to him.

In this example, the helplessness had both predisposing and precipitating factors. The candidate was young, away from home, and suffering the first crisis of independent existence. The only family structure that had been present, the relationship with the girlfriend, had been severed by her rejection of his advances.

Depressed, forlorn, and crying, psychologically he was in the condition of the helpless infant. The God Experience, the propensity for which had been laid down since infancy, happened. It was similar to so many other episodes reported by the religious. The impact influenced the rest of his life.

Sometimes helplessness can be less acute. It can creep up on the person slowly, gradually, until a single unimportant thing precipitates the experience, the straw that breaks the camel's back. The most typical slow, creeping type of helplessness is aging.

This kind of helplessness has many symptoms that include: boredom with the job and family, the failure to obtain basic stimulation from living, the resurrection of the adolescent obsession that there must be something more to life, and the sensation that time is flying by. Components of each of these sensations are correlates of the aging crisis.

Perhaps the single most significant factor that precipitates this type of helplessness is physical change. In addition to wrinkles in the face and gray streaks in the hair, the body appears to slow down. The person gains weight, loses muscle strength, and no longer has the spryness of a 20-year-old.

There is no escape. No matter what the person does, aging continues. The body becomes weaker and the aspirations of a lifetime are seen as illusions. Novelty loses its thrill and all the things that might have been are lost in the everyday humdrum. Sooner or later the possibility of death enters the picture.

There are stages in the reaction to aging. These are similar to those of acute life-endangering situations and, interestingly enough, to the separation anxiety of the infant. When a child is separated from its mother for the first long period of time, three stages are evident.

The first is called the protest stage. During this period, the child screams, cries, and raises general havoc. This behavior continues for hours to days, depending on the number of times the child has been separated from the mother in the past. Then suddenly, the child stops crying.

It enters the second stage; depression. During this time, the child does not cry, but just lies in bed. Appetite is depressed and a general lethargy is evident. The child appears to have given up. After a few hours to days, more or less normal behaviors occur once again. It appears that the child has recuperated. However, when the mother returns, the child ignores her. To her surprise, he does not respond to her in any meaningful way. Sometimes it barely acknowledges her existence.

The adult's response to the concept of life is very similar. First, as the individual realizes that life is a terminal condition and that death is the ultimate reality, the protest stage begins. The person vocalizes repeatedly, "Why me? Why not the next person? Why do we have to die? Why can't I live forever?" In terminal patients, who know their deaths are imminent, the behavior can approach frank irritability.

The anticipation of a sudden end to life is frustrating and prone to producing aggression. This frustrative aggression is aimed at the source of the frustration, life itself. People say they hate life or that life is "the pits" or that life is an illusion. The aggression is turned toward life or its most obvious symbol, youth. Young people receive the brunt of hatred.

Then, after one final flurry, the aggression stops. The once complaining person becomes quiet. He or she sits in the room and stares at the wall. Occasionally, a few words are mumbled. Friends and neighbors become concerned about the deterioration in the person's behavior.

Some people in this stage become autistic. They don't move, or they rock back and forth in the dark. They may become bedridden and develop a series of "progressive" disorders. In short, they become psychologically helpless.

Depending on the learning history, the strong expectation develops that *someone will come*. The person begins to read "scriptures" and suddenly finds another understanding. During the night, a "soft voice" comes from within the head and says, "I am the lamb of God" or "I am the alpha and the omega."

The change that follows is highly variable. Some individuals suddenly return to church, especially if this behavior was learned when they were very young, and find new meaning. Other individuals, without a history of churchgoing become more transcendental or mystical. God has special significance to them. They set aside a part of their house or a portion of their schedule to have a personal communion.

Regardless of the form of the change, the orientation to life is similar. Like the young child who no longer appears interested in its mother when she returns after separation, life is seen as a transient thing. It was nice, but it's not everything. There is more to life—an eternal life, with the eternal abstract of God.

7
Word Games: The Semantics of Anxiety and Anxiety Reduction

A popular childhood defense to taunts is, "Sticks and stones may break my bones, but names will never hurt me." If one is referring to physical injury, this statement may be true. However, if one is referring to emotional or psychological damage, then this cliché is definitely in error.

Words are extraordinarily powerful stimuli to which we all respond. The consequences of hearing a relative say, "Your mother has just died" is sufficient to produce both short- and long-term changes in your behavior. Just a simple sentence, when the words are right, can drive the body into periods of grief, or terror, or intense anxiety.

They can be positive stimuli as well. There are few methods more effective than being told you are loved for raising the emotions to euphoria. Simple statements, such as, "You look good today" or "Aren't you looking radiant" have been known to maintain a person's positive self-image for hours, sometimes days.

Words are potent controllers of our behavior. Their power is so pervasive that we are often caught unaware by the illusions they create. We forget that words are simple verbal utterances or scratches of lines on a piece of paper. They are substitutions, indeed forgeries, of direct experiences.

By themselves, words are meaningless sounds emitted from the voice box or whispered to ourselves as "thoughts." By themselves, sentences are slashes in mud or cuneiform tablets or trails of graphite on a sheet of wood pulp. They can be as nonsensical as the first exposure to any foreign language.

Words become meaningful when they are paired with particular experiences. Sentences and paragraphs become understandable only when they follow rules generalized from experience. The relationship between words and objects or events is a function of learning and early reinforcement history. There is nothing special about calling one object "cup" and another "father"; the association is purely arbitrary. The opposite could just as easily be true. The association depends on what objects and words have been paired.

Words are constructs for the complex events that occur, second after second, within individual experience. They must be understood as being distinct from the objects they designate. Statements are not proofs by virtue of the fact that they can be said or written.

The frequency of a sequence of words does not necessarily reflect its validity. If a young child is taught to say the word "cup" in the presence of its mother, it will say "cup" more and more frequently whenever the mother is present. The young child may mature and continue to call the mother "cup." It makes no difference whether the word is repeated once or thousands of times, the mere usage of a word or a phrase does not demonstrate its validity. From the perspective of the English language, the child is still mistaken. The object with the familiar shape, particular smells, and inexhaustible warmth, is called some variant of "mother."

Obviously either word is arbitrary. There is no empirical reason why the child could not call the mother a "cup." As long as the same word was systematically and logically used, the warm woman could be called a "cup."

Yet, despite the arbitrary and relative nature of language, people still become obsessed by the illusions of repetition. Many people believe that the number of repetitions, of either words or actions, are direct proofs of their validity. This presumption is blatant in statements such as, "Hundreds of generations have said that there is eternal life."

Repetition can be an index of experience; however, it is not an index of accuracy or validity. It is just as likely that the person may have been repeating the same error for ten years. It is just as probable that the person has been calling an object by an inappropriate word for 20 years. Erroneous responses can be displayed just as frequently as correct ones.

Time is hardly a proof of validity or accuracy. The fact that hundreds of generations have lived by the same belief does not necessarily demonstrate its validity. For thousands of years people thought the world was flat. Such a statement had been made hundreds of thousands of times, despite the fact that the earth is *not* flat. People once thought that ball lightning and other odd displays in nature were signs of departed spirits. Rich mythologies were built around the occurrence of bright lights and thunderstorms. But ball lightning was found to be another manifestation of the principles of electromagnetism.

The frequency of words by itself does not change natural events. One can argue, thousands of times, that you will float when you walk off the top of a building. But no matter how frequently the phrase is repeated, you will fall at the rate of 32 feet per second per second. Now, you may not feel this effect (in fact the last thing you may remember before you smash into the ground is the sensation of floating), but other people and nonsubjective instruments will indicate the fall.

Much has been written in the history of science in response to new discoveries. When religious people of the sixteenth century were shocked by the discovery that the earth was *not* the center of the solar system, they protested for decades. Poets and religious teachers alike lamented, and wrote, time after time, that the earth is a special creation, the center of the universe.

Subsequent generations forgot these bursts of frustration. The failures of repetition as a proof of validity fade into the past. A historian of science may occasionally find old explanations on some dusty shelf, still fresh with the conviction that frequent repetition is the only measure of truth. Such beliefs persist today.

What has changed are the belief systems that are being defended. People now realize that no matter how many times they say that the sun revolves around the earth, that this is not so. The experience is an illusion of the *perceptual reference*, a kind of egocentric measurement error.

Today, people still believe that the mere statement "God exists" is proof that a supreme being *must* be there, somewhere. In fact, the more frequently the statement is repeated, the more convinced some people become that God must exist. This is no more useful than people insisting that the world is flat or repeatedly denying the observation that it is round.

Words written on tablets, books, or parchment also tend to command a sense of validity. Unlike the spoken language, which is heard and then quickly disappears, written language is there to be viewed repeatedly. As old arguments and clever phrases fade into the past, the written word remains.

Consequently, there is a great tendency to use written words as proof. How many times have you heard the unenlightened argument, "It must be so because I read it in a book," or "It must be true because I read it somewhere." Truth is not proven simply because some words are written down. Reaching a conclusion requires much more sophisticated techniques.

Testaments handed down for centuries do not prove the validity of what they contend. They only indicate that ideas have been around for quite a while, like the human brain. The fact that a writer of another time, much less educated than the contemporary average person, said that "God exists" does not add any more assurance that God existed then than it does now. It is no more valid than arguing that birdmen actually existed merely because they were drawn on the wall of an ancient burial chamber.

Sure there are the evasions, the verbal tricks by which the faithful circumvent the problem. They can argue that the author of the testament—John, Moses, Joseph Smith, Muhammad, Buddha—was chosen. You can say that his or her message was "inspired," even though objective measurement indicates no difference between the semantic patterns of holy literature and those of the secular writing of the same period.

Without objective measurement and careful confirmation, there are no measures of verbal validity. Without the capacity to *quantitatively predict* and to refute the endless numbers of options, there is no possibility of concrete determination.

The occasional guess and general statement is expected to be correct by chance alone. When scholars read the Old Testament and determine the location of Sodom and Gomorrah, the detection of these cities proves only that they were there. No matter how many times you read the scripture, it does not prove the claims that Sodom and Gomorrah were destroyed by God's wrath. It is no more valid than the supposition that the city of Lisbon was destroyed by demons. Today, we call them earthquakes.

Vast numbers of people reporting an experience do not add to its validity. That an observation of saints and gods in the sky was reported by 30,000 people during the year 1917 does not prove the accuracy of the report. When a camera records only a bright light and later investigation shows the event was a simple extension of natural laws, faithful statements become empty words.

The experiences of God during a crisis by untold millions of people do not prove his existence. The belief that one must have a crisis in order to know that God exists does not prove he is there; indeed, it may only indicate that under conditions of stress, human brains behave in similar ways.

And last of all, frequency of denial does not alter the probability of things. No matter how many times you state, "I will not die," you will still die, ultimately. You can waffle on this issue, and say that "a part of you" lives on or endures for centuries until Judgment Day. You can also state some things (like souls) are spiritual and not bound by physical principle. But these are statements without an actual referent. No matter how many times you repeat them, their truth is not proven.

However, words are powerful controllers of human behavior. Millions of people have felt better because someone said, "You will not die, but will live forever." Generations have lived according to a golden rule because it had written that they would be rewarded for following a path of righteousness.

There is something very powerful about the process of language. Every human culture that has been reported by anthropologists has special sequences of words (or thoughts) that contain properties by which the person allegedly can heal, procure food, or obtain eternal life. Usually these special words must be said in a particular sequence, in a specific setting, and in a passive mode.

Prayers are special Christian words. Immortality (in some form) can be achieved by saying sequences such as, "God save me" or "In the name of Christ, I believe." Islamic phrases are just as fixed in their required form. The believer thinks he can obtain special dispensations by saying words like "Allah is the only God" or "Allah be praised."

The source of the alleged power of words is tied to the inseparable interaction between the growth of the self-concept and the development of language. Whether the concept of self emerged first within the human species and language came later or vice versa is not relevant here. The critical factor is that they appear to have evolved at about the same time. (There also may be a *third factor* responsible for both the development of the self-concept and the emergence of language. Such a factor is evident in each growing child.)

Regardless of the "causes" (if indeed this question is a legitimate one), the intimate relationships between thinking, language, and the self-concept have given the human species an interesting property. We live in a world of words.

Words, whether they are spoken or read, are the means by which we relive old experiences. Long after the first love is dead, we rekindle it by reading the vivid sequences of youth in bloom. Long after memories have faded, we rekindle the original luster by reading old diaries or listening to childhood stories once again.

Through learning, our emotions become tied to words and word sequences. A sequence of four letters can induce revulsion and disgust in some people, but produce joy and anticipation in others. A simple sentence like "You will die" can induce terror in some individuals but herald the culmination of a lifelong dream for others.

Through conditioning, our concept of self is tied to words. You label parts of your body with various words. You talk to other people in words. In fact, you scheme, plan, swear, and remember with words. You call your "self" by words. And sometimes, inflated and unrealistic, you even define yourself by words.

By using the predicate form, "I am ______," the simplest form of association, the concept of self becomes connected to groups. Insult to the group is experienced as an insult to the individual. For example, if you have said, "I am an American" many times, then the occurrence of "American" elicits the idea of "I." Consequently, when someone says, "All Americans are loud and stupid," you become angry. If you have said, "I am a Canadian" throughout your life and someone says, "Canadians are U.S. lackeys," this, too, would be interpreted as "fightin' words."

The conditioning is often subtle or passive. You may not actively think of yourself as a welder, construction worker, office manager, or politician—it's just a job. But after a few hundred indirect answers to the question, "What do you do for a living?" the associations become stronger. You find yourself becoming angry merely because someone says, "I hear construction workers are a bunch of uneducated rednecks," or "Professors are perverts."

Most of the time, you say the words to yourself. There is little difference between the principles associated with using words overtly and using them as thoughts. The primary distinction is that, unlike public words, you are the only one that has direct access to this private conversation. Unlike your liver chemistry, heart rate or brain waves, which (technically) could be viewed by many other people, only the "experiencer" has access to his or her private responses (Holland 1981). They are inseparably woven into the concept of the self.

With an almost imperceptible movement of the larynx or voice box, you "talk" to yourself when you are alone. During emotional crisis, when your lover leaves or a close relative dies, you create long, eloquent soliloquies about yourself, life, and the universe. Long after the embarrassing confrontation has ceased, you spend periods of private time concocting convoluted conversations that you wish you had said.

Since each of us is immersed in an infinite sequence of words and thoughts, it is not suprising that they would be perceived as having special properties. Words are not like the objects they represent. Human beings cannot control the seasons, the delivery of important rewards, the occurrence of adversity, or the manifestation of joy. We can modify their presentations, by building structures; we can use our brains to avoid negative consequences. However, most important environmental events are still beyond our individual control.

We do appear to control our thoughts. We *appear* to manipulate our private words and sentences. They are within our grasp. For a moment, even the absolute barrier of death can be breached and the loved one is seen in the mind's eye as if yesterday were now. These properties have often given the impression that thoughts are different from other "things." Even though specific thoughts are consequences of learning language, the thinker is pressed by the conviction that they are nonphysical. They do not appear to be like vocal utterances.

Considering the powerful control of language over human experience, one should know the limitations of this behavior. Are there built-in flaws within language itself? Are there quirks and peculiarities in combinations of words that induce false problems and create artificial hopes? After all, there is nothing sacred about human language. The capacity to deal with complicated sequences of syllables emerged as a consequence of or in correlation with the development of Broca's and Wernicke's areas within the brain. It was built on the universal associative capacity displayed by all animal life, from the single-celled amoeba to the trillion-celled human primate.

There is an implicit principle within the methodology of science. It states that one should know the limitation of the measurement device; one should clearly understand the validity of the recording procedure. Without this knowledge, which is often difficult to obtain by simple observation, foolish and sometimes dangerous conclusions can be made. Can you imagine the errors that would abound in physics, for example, if scientists did not realize that the internal wiring of a device used to measure the intensity of magnetic fields could be directly influenced by those fields? Without that knowledge, an inaccurate conclusion would be made about the presence of magnetic fields near the sensor when they were actually influencing the instrument itself.

Can you imagine the misinterpretations that would proliferate in chemistry if the warm-up time for an instrument was considered to be a part of the phenomenon being measured? If the needle on the instrument jumped wildly back and forth because of the basic construction of the apparatus, the unwary experimenter would conclude that the fluctuation was some property of the phenomenon being studied. She would not realize that it was a fluke in the instrument's construction.

Language, too, has built-in peculiarities. Like any other measurement procedure, language processes have quirks and limitations that must be recognized. Unfortunately, most of these oddities have been used to buttress belief systems and to prove the existence of phenomena that are not there. Since the concept of self is so intricately embedded within the nature of language, the deception is difficult to determine.

The most challenging consequence of realizing the limits of language and the flukes of thinking is that *some phenomena may be purely creations of human language itself.* In other words, these phenomena are created by the capability of displaying this behavior rather than by being represented by it. Religious behaviors and proofs are notorious candidates for this category.

There are three features of language that are immediately relevant to religious behaviors and to the verbal support of the God Experience. The first is the failure to recognize the distinction between concrete and abstract words. The second error lies in the inability to realize that not all questions have answers. The third feature is an illusion more than an error; it depends on the inability to prove that something doesn't exist.

Essentially, there are two types of words: those that have empirical referents and those that do not. By empirical referent, I mean the word refers to something that can be measured directly; it is publicly verifiable. Classic examples are *chair*, *mother*, *book*, *beer bottle*, or *Millennium Falcon*. It makes little difference whether the words refer to an object or a process, as long as the referent is measurable. Sample processes include "a moving car," "a roundhouse kick to the head," or "someone making an ass out of himself." They are all quite discrete and empirical occurrences that refer to actions.

Words with empirical referents are usually learned in the presence of the object. For example, you first learned the word *cat* when you saw the furry, purring object that suddenly began swishing its tail when you pulled its ears. You first learned the word *move* when the toy truck rolled across the floor.

So far there is no difficulty. Words that refer to empirical referents have clear consensus. Most everyone will agree, after the word *cat* has been paired with the appropriate object, that something either was or was not a cat. The word is a simple substitution for a very obvious object.

But now the problems begin. Words with nonempirical referents are quite different both in terms of the way in which they are learned and their effects on behavior. A list of nonempirical words might include *God*, *eternity*, *infinity*, and *love*. In the past, the words *electron* and *gene* could have been included as well.

These words are not learned in the presence of any particular object or process, since they do not refer to anything that is measurable. Some of these words might also be called "abstracts" in a very general sense. They are *assumed* to refer to things that exist but cannot be immediately seen in their entirety.

The term *personality* is a good example. It refers to the thousands of responses that a person might display in hundreds of situations over many decades. Instead of describing every detail of an immense space-time pattern of responses, within one small human locus, we use an abstract: "personality."

Certainly, it is not precise. We cannot predict anything about the specific person simply by using the word. We would have to measure, quantitatively, the relationships between the many responses. However, the word does refer to something that *could be* directly measurable and publicly verifiable.

Abstract words can be useful in inferring what *may* be there. It's a type of "where there's smoke, there's fire" logic. If enough events occur that seem to represent the operation of some other thing (that you cannot presently measure), then you use a word for it. An abstract approach was helpful for pursuing the concept of an electron before it was measured directly. Repeated measurements were made that indicated that something was there. This thing could not be immediately detected, only inferred.

However, not all nonempirical words are created equally. There is a great difference between a nonempirical word like *electron* or *gene* (before DNA was discovered) and nonempirical words like *eternity*, *God*, or *infinity*. This difference is often overlooked because of the confusion between verbal and numerical statements. Whereas the characteristics of the electron became more obvious as more measurements were taken, nonempirical words like *God* do not benefit from any measurement. No matter how many measurements are taken, one is no closer to the solution of the problem or to the detection of the alleged phenomenon's characteristics than before.

God words are analogous to the warm-up fluctuations in the needle of the instrument in the chemistry lab. Unlike the other fluctuations on the needle that are associated with actual phenomena, God Experiences cannot be verified and extended. They are a part of the machine, a part of the language process.

Of course, I am not implying that the same words function to satisfy the flukes of language and the artifacts of the brain's construction. There is nothing magical about the word *God*; it is simply dog spelled backwards.

Words like *God*, *Allah*, or the *Great Cosmic Whole* are catchall terms for ideas on conceptual limits of space and time. More esoteric (and idiosyncratic) substitutions include "the human spirit," "*n*th dimension," and some variant of "the eternal collective consciousness of humanity." The critical feature is the symbolic function rather than the spelling.

But if these words are really flukes of human language (regardless of the content) and artifacts of the human brain's capacity to symbolically represent time and space, why are they maintained (often eagerly)? Wouldn't these words, sooner or later, be seen as a sham?

Their persistence lies, first of all, in the fact that all human cultures must have child-rearing practices through which everyone must pass. If there were no parent–child relationships, the young human being would not live to be an adult. God words are symbolic extensions of these concrete childhood experiences into the adult world of words and abstract reasoning.

The second cause lies in the nature of nonempirical words themselves. Unlike words that refer to empirical events or objects, the concepts associated with nonempirical words are difficult to extinguish. In this instance, "extinguish'' means the word is no longer associated with the presence of the object or process to which it has been paired.

If an empirical word is inappropriate, then the consequences are clear. When the child uses the word ''dog'' in the presence of a furry object that purrs, the effect is obvious. The object is very discrete in time and space (and hence is easily perceived) and the word is simply not appropriate. The parents say, ''No, this is a cat.''

God words do not refer to any particular empirical referent. Their meaning has been achieved by nonspecific clustering of a variety of different and usually emotionally loaded associations. It starts subtly with predicate forms such as ''God is love,'' ''God is life,'' or ''God is good, God is great.'' By this simple pairing, all of the diffuse, positive responses associated with the words *love*, *life*, *good*, and *great* are transferred to the nonsense word *God*.

The next step of the conditioning occurs by pairing God with words that represent the upper boundaries of space and time. Statements like ''God created everything'' or ''God is infinite'' are typical implicit chains. The verbal human animal is forced to conclude that God is omnipresent and omnipotent. As a result, there is no way in which to extinguish the word; there is no way to refute, to specify, or to point to referents. Because of the pairings with the word, just about everything the person experiences appears to be an indirect proof of its validity.

Gradually, God words (including *eternity* and *infinity*) begin to acquire the status of words that have empirical referents. As more and more indirect associations become paired with God words, they appear more and more real. Finally, the person concludes that the word *must refer to a real thing*.

This conviction usually elicits the second problem of language: the presumption that failure to prove a negative is proof that it is there. This simple idea is expressed in many forms. The most common phrase is, ''How do you know that God does not exist?'' The verbally naive who use this form of proof assume that the failure to answer the question is a demonstration that the question is valid. However, the exercise is a word game, since *nothing* can really be proven not to exist; it's a limit of the instrument—language.

For example, I could argue that the universe was created by invisible, nonphysical pink elephants. Because these elephants formed the universe, they created the largest living land animal in their own image. Furthermore, they gave earth elephants ivory so that they would be preyed on by two-legged parasites who would kill them for this godly gift; this would be a test of faith.

You may not like my idea of creation. You might think that the idea of nonphysical, invisible pink elephants is absurd. But you cannot prove they don't exist. Such a proof would require you to measure the entire universe (space) for as long as it existed (time). Even if you completed this mammoth task (theoretically, of course), you would not have gained a thing. If you look carefully at my statement, I said that these were *nonphysical*, *invisible* pink elephants. By defining them that way, I have completely eliminated the possibility that you could ever measure them, even if they did exist. How can you measure something that is nonphysical?

Put simply, you cannot measure something that is nonphysical because it does not exist, except as a word. It can never exist, except as a word. Certainly, things may exist that are not *yet* detectable, but they are not nonphysical. The term *nonphysical* indicates that, by (very arbitrary) definition, it can never be detected.

Nonphysical is a first cousin to words that always evoke the answer "n + 1." One popular game has been to ask, "What is the smallest piece of matter?" Because of the nature of language, measurement of smaller and smaller components always elicits the expectation that there is *still* something smaller. This apparently infinite progression is an illusion produced by a semantic do-loop. One can move around a circle for an indefinite time without going anywhere.

By now, you should see the nature of this word game. You should appreciate the stupidity of using "You can't prove it's not there" as support for anything. But for those of you who still think the universe was not created by invisible, nonphysical pink elephants—prove they are not there.

The God argument is no different. Since this word is defined as something that is spiritual (nonphysical and invisible), there is no way you could ever refute it. Incidentally, there is also no way you could ever prove it.

These kinds of questions evoke the third and final major problem of using language as a support for God Experiences. It reflects the subtle consequences not of specific words but of *patterns of words*. Perhaps the most important pattern is that of the question, which produces the expectation of an answer. If, for several days, I presented a cup of coffee to you and then, a few seconds later, gave you some doughnuts, the two events would become paired. Soon you would expect that for every cup of coffee, a doughnut should follow. This expectation is a consequence of conditioning.

Throughout our verbal lives, we are exposed to a similar conditioned pattern of expectation. Like the doughnut following the coffee, we begin to anticipate an answer to every question. Year after year, we are taught to expect a response to any series of words cast within a question format.

This stimulus–response pattern is acquired like the association between words and objects. The major difference is that since we use word sequences to talk and to think for long periods of time, we cannot easily see the subtleties of these patterns. They are beyond the limits of our sense of present. But they are certainly there.

It starts with the first questions as when the child asks, "What is this?" and the parent says, "This is a fork." The pattern is then strengthened by more abstract references such as, "Why is the sky blue?" and the answer is, "Go ask your mother." Regardless of the consequences, correct or erroneous, the question is paired with an answer.

Some questions do *not* have sensical answers. For all practical purposes, they do not have any answers at all. This is especially true for questions that contain words for which there are no empirical referents. How many angels can dance on the head of a pin? What is the sound of one hand clapping? Do you walk to school or take your lunch? Although they are nonsense questions (now), people have spent (and some still spend) hundreds of hours trying to find the answers.

Because of the endless repetition of question–answer pairing (how many times in your life have you asked a question?), the expectation of answers is hard to contain. For example, I could ask, "Where do unicorns come from?" and you might say, "Unicorns don't exist." But then you'll walk away and at some point might also ask, "I know they don't exist, but suppose they did—where *would* they come from?"

Less obvious nonsense questions arise when *inaccurate* words are used in a question format. One of the most common examples, a kind of mixed metaphor, is the sequence frequently used by the Jehovah's Witnesses as an implicit proof of God. The sequence is, "Who creates a house?" Answer: "Man." Then, "Who creates man?"

The unwary thinker, seduced into the semantic trap, attempts to answer the question in that format or set. Who did create man? Within that context, the person is not likely to realize that the word "create" is heavily loaded by the presumption of being constructed in a human sense. It assumes that humanity was made and did not happen, emerge, evolve, or occur by some as yet unknown process. The reader is caught before he can escape. Religious proofs are frequently based on these types of word games. They are intended to befuddle. They capitalize on the compulsion to complete semantic closure, to finish a question with an answer.

Perhaps the most pressing series of questions that compel semantic closure are the nascence themes. Classic formats are: "How large is the universe?" "How was the universe formed?" For those who are more egocentric and project their human traits on nature, the question is usually cast as, "*Who* created the universe?" People who ask these questions implicitly assume that there must be an answer. They may believe technology will be available someday to deliver the long-sought solution. They do not realize that they may be asking not only the wrong question, but a nonsensical one as well.

So who cares about word games? Why not leave them to philosophers and psychologists and to people that are clever with words? If language were some instrument that we could use and set aside, that suggestion would be appropriate. Games are clever diversions but not labors for serious consideration.

The problem is that thinking and the basic concept of self are tied to words. If there are flukes and artifacts in words or their patterns, then these peculiarities will also emerge in our thinking. These oddities will be manifested, indeed embedded, within the concept of self.

This power can be seen in the final contribution of language to the human insistence on God answers. Language both mediates and creates anxiety. Just a few simple symbols like "You have cancer" can induce panic and anxiety. They can be just as disrupting as actual pain.

Anxiety is a private experience. It occupies the interval between the presentation of a cue that has been paired with a negative stimulus and the later occurrence of that stimulus. Anxiety does not occur in the presence of the negative stimulus itself; such later emotions are usually called *fear*. In such a situation, the stimulus is obvious and discrete. Anxiety is the anticipation, the foreboding, the extrapolation that something "bad" will happen. Physiological studies cleary indicate that anxiety can evoke more severe body changes than the effects of the negative stimulus itself. The old statement, "There is nothing to fear but fear itself" is all about anxiety.

A number of different negative stimuli can be sources of anxiety. The most well-known class of events involves pain. If a father's frown is frequently followed a few minutes later by a slap in the face, the frown becomes a cue for the anticipation of the slap. The experience between the frown and the slap is characterized by anxiety. Ongoing responses, including thinking and talking, are suppressed.

A second class of anxiety stimuli involves simple deviations from expectation, especially if the expectation involves negative possibilities. If you are paid once a week for your services, a sudden change in the payment schedule can be associated with anxiety. The change is a clear deviation from the expectation of reward.

A final class of stimuli involves the strange and the unknown. These stimuli become cues for the possibility that some other unknown thing can occur. Since strange and unknown events are paired with frightening and potentially harmful consequences, they, too, can become sources of anxiety.

Human beings shun unpredictability. They pursue any ritual that will ensure the certainty (the accurate prediction) of basic rewards such as food and warmth. They concoct any series of words that will reduce the terror of the unknown. They adhere to explanations even though they have absolutely no relevance to the phenomenon in question.

If the book in front of you suddenly floated above your head and flew across the room, you would feel a slight sense of stimulation. Some people would be afraid, and a few would think of some label, like "poltergeist," for weird events. A couple readers wouldn't even notice.

However, if I then said it was all due to "hypnotism," most of you would heave a sigh of relief and say, "Oh, I see." Even though the word *hypnotism* tells you absolutely nothing about how the phenomenon occurred, you might feel relieved. Even though the explanation gives you no information to predict the phenomenon, you would sit there with a sense of quiet understanding.

Language fosters every source of anxiety. It contains words for extrapolation of pain to the concept of self (*death* and *annihilation*). With the simple sequence, "I will die," language can form perhaps the most terrifying anxiety paradigm of all: the anticipation of personal demise.

In this translation of a simple reinforcement schedule into a language sequence, the word *die* becomes the negative stimulus. The word itself receives its meaning by previous pairings with dead things and the pain associated with parents' or others' statements, such as, "Do you want to *die*? You will, if you cut yourself again."

The person's conceptual stage of development affects the perception of death; descriptions change with age. Young children, who are dying from leukemia, for example, perceive death as a kind of separation anxiety from the parents. Older children, under ten years of age, appear to fear the pain associated with the death process.

Once an abstract concept of space and time has been acquired after age 12 or 13 (on the average), death is connected to the dissolution of the self. However, individuals who place great emphasis on appearance (some adult females in particular), may pair with the anxiety of deterioration and rotting of the body. Like everything else, the images of death words are a function of experience.

The anticipation, the semantic equivalent of time, is the future tense of the verb *to be*. This word symbolizes the fact that the negative stimulus *will* occur in the future. The cues are many, from simply watching birthdays slowly accumulate to noting old friends passing away. The target of the effect, the "I," is obvious.

Language also generates anxiety through its own limitations. There are certain questions that deviate from expectation; they do not appear to have any answers. The questions "Where will I go when I die?" and "What is eternity like?" are not immediately followed by answers. Semantic closure is violated and anxiety occurs. To eliminate the gnawing anticipation that would ultimately incapacitate even the most hearty atheist, an inevitable sequence of thinking begins. The more it occurs, the more the anxiety is reduced. The more the anxiety is reduced, the more the sequence occurs. It is so simple that a first-year psychology student could derive it, once the operation was demonstrated. There are two stages.

The first response involves the elimination of the anxiety. Since the existential anxiety is due to the sequence "I will die," it can be extinguished by "defusing" the semantics. Different human cultures have attacked different parts of this deadly sequence.

The first technique is to eliminate the negative stimulus of death. The person can claim, "I will not die," or simply insist that death does not exist. However, the latter case does not correspond with actual observation, since people continue to die and disintegrate in their places of deposition.

At this point, the importance of the semantic self becomes apparent. The intimate connection between language and the experience of self is manifested. The person concludes that the "I" is not the same as "the body"; it is the body that dies and not the "I."

It is a necessary conclusion. Slowly, as millions of sentences and thought sequences are experienced in a lifetime, the person learns that the body does not appear to be totally correlated with the self. There are times, after all, when one cannot control the body, such as during sickness or fatigue. And, there are times when the body does not appear to control the "I."

Since thoughts are different from words and outside objects, they *appear* to follow other laws. One appears to be able to influence one's own thoughts, whereas events and objects in the environment are more difficult to control. At the end of this logic lies the source of the soul–body dichotomy.

A second approach is to eliminate the "I" component of the problem. Instead of concentrating on the "die" aspect of the paradigm "I will die," eliminate the "I." This is completed in a very effective way: by simply stating that the "I" does not exist.

This approach is more popular among some Asian religions. By stating that the "I" is an illusion, an artifact of learning language, the sentence "I will die" is no longer meaningful. If there is no locus at which to anticipate the delivery of the negative stimulus, then there is no anxiety.

Obviously, this approach is not very popular is Western culture, where great emphasis is placed on the individual. After a lifetime of fostering egocentrism and emphasizing the boundaries of the body and the self, this approach would not eliminate the death anxiety. If anything, it would probably increase it.

The final approach, an odd and esoteric one, is to concentrate on the verb "will" of the sentence. Anxiety only occurs during anticipation. By eliminating "will" (that is, by saying that death does not occur in the future but is occurring now), anxiety is reduced.

This approach to the perennial problem is interesting, since it states that death is happening all the time. The minute you are born you are dead. The cessation of the self is a minor punctuation of a lifelong process. Although the idea generates some aversion, there is less anxiety.

People who have been conditioned to think in terms of the first solution, to deny or eliminate the aversive stimulus (death), must utilize the second stage of the "survival logic." At some point, the question rises, "If I do survive bodily death, then what *is* there?" The absence of information about what there is becomes another form of unpredictability and fear.

Some cultures concentrate on the simplest solution to this semantic stress. They eliminate totally the implication of an end. Reincarnation explanations serve this function by stating that the "self" never dies but keeps recycling. There is no end in such a circle, and no anxiety.

Still other cultures have attempted to eliminate the anxiety of the unknown by giving convenient structures to the anticipated event. The Tibetan Book of the Dead (Evans-Wentz 1972), for example, contains a series of expectations and explanations for what the person will encounter once death has occurred. It makes no difference whether or not these explanations are correct. In fact, they could be complete fantasies and merely reflect the specific experiences of people in that part of the world. The critical feature is that they eliminate death anxiety by reducing uncertainty.

The fact that similar allusions to death (from people who have almost died) exist in many human cultures does not prove the validity of these experiences. Similar *near-death reports may only reflect the similar construction of the human brain*. They may indicate only that human brains undergo similar sequences as bodies slowly die.

This is certainly not surprising and would even be mundane if any other part of the human body was involved. Manifestations of muscle deterioration, for example, follow more or less the same sequence no matter what human culture has reported it.

But then what happens? Once one dies and passes through various stages or "journeys," some end must come sooner or later. What is at this end? The thinker is faced again with the anxiety of termination.

At this point, God words become critical. They do not have specific references or imply the properties of termination. God words are paired with the concepts of timelessness and infinity.

God words are the ultimate and final solution to the existential anxiety of survival. For example, if something, be it labeled "God," "Yahweh," "Allah," or "the Great Cosmic Whole," is never-ending, then anxiety does not occur. There is no anticipation because the end can *never* happen.

How can the person achieve the properties of this nonanxious concept? How can the semantic self become a thing that will live forever? The stage is set for the final, predictable, and ultimate semantic sequence. It is completed in a single stroke.

The person simply says or thinks, "I believe in God," or "I am a child of God." Through this easy paired association in semantic space, the characteristics of God words are generalized to the concept of the self.

As long as the God concept is never challenged, anxiety is reduced forever. Space becomes irrelevant. The terror of being a diminutive thing in the context of an incomprehensible, unfathomable universe dissolves. Time does not exist. Eternity is the only alternative.

The second stage is a predictable sequence of events. Again, it makes no difference whether or not God exists. It is irrelevant that God words are artifacts of human language and convenient constructs for the limits of space and time. The critical feature is the consequence; the reduction of anxiety. If the anxiety of self-annihilation is reduced after the person says, "I am a child of God," then the statement will be made more and more frequently.

These consequences start a chain reaction. As the response "I am a child of God" is repeated, more and more God associations are recruited. Father images, abstract impressions, and deep affective tones are strengthened. Old childhood responses, long repressed by the world of logic and rationality, stir again.

Powered by the sudden cessation of lifelong anxiety, the association bursts into consciousness like a supernova. An unending sequence of bright and significant God signs inundate awareness. Due to their sheer numbers and sudden appearance, they become a compelling point of focus.

There are many labels for this sudden rebound. People have called these experiences "conversions," "seeing the light," and "cosmic understanding." Whatever the phrases used, the event is always characterized by sudden inspiration that appears instantaneous. It is similar to insight learning.

This crystallization of "what it's all about" is correlated with an affective experience as well. The sudden overshoot induces a wave of joy and peak elation followed by a sense of serenity and cosmic quiescence. It is similar to, although magnitudes greater than, the serenity that follows when the child receives the long-awaited punishment and cries itself to sleep.

As the occurrence of God words reduce anxiety, they become more and more powerful. Everyday events are explained within the new context. All uncertainties are cast in this connection. People die "because it's God's will." Unusual things happen "because it's Allah's will." No matter what happens, it is "His" will. There is no uncertainty and no anxiety. The semantic structure is complete.

However, God words must have certain properties to fulfill the role of an anxiety reducer. Without these properties, they would not contain the potential to eliminate the anticipation and, consequently, the concept would not be rewarded.

The first property of God words has been discussed. They must imply infinity and eternity. Such associations cannot be extinguished, since the referents can never be in one place or exist long enough to be punished.

The second property is that God words must be simple. Procedures by which heavenly rewards can be obtained must be routine and easily discriminable. If they are not, then the procedures themselves could induce anxiety. Very convoluted and difficult "means" of obtaining God words are tantamount to insoluble problems. They lead to uncertainty and the possibility of finite conditions. There is also the possibility that you may not solve the problem.

Effective God words are obtained by simple requests like "God save me." They must be available at the last minute just before the plane crashes, the car slams into a wall, or the last semblance of awareness fades into oblivion. In Christianity, for example, even a person who has lived "in sin" can be "saved" if he or she calls on Christ as a mediator.

The third property of God words is their association with the past. Although the anxiety of death can be eliminated by believing there is no death, references to the past are important. The past has occurred. There is no anxiety there (real or anticipated), since it has already happened. Consequently, God words that are very old and have been used repeatedly over the centuries are preferable to new God words.

The fourth property of God words is the persistence of metaphors; God words are embedded in metaphors. They are useful semantic tools because they invoke rich images and profound affective experiences without defining the issue specifically. Metaphors or parables are so general that they can be meaningful to anyone.

For example, the metaphor "God's goodness flows into the soul of man" can generate an unending stream of associations (the effect is similar to the free association that you catch yourself displaying just before you fall asleep at night). In this instance, the word "flow" implies a river. It contains water. Water can be seen as a liquid, a solid, or a gas. Rivers can be good or bad, depending on the human behavior involved. The river can both give and take life away. No matter how many human generations live and die beside it, the river continues to flow. It is always changing, yet it is always the same.

So on and on, literally and figuratively, it goes. Up to a point, the more unusual metaphors are the most effective. They generate long periods of "novel" thought sequences. One classic example is, "Yea, though I walk through the valley of the shadow of death, I will fear no evil. . . . " The conjunction of the associations of "valley" (a discrete referent) and "shadow of death" (which attributes concrete characteristics to an abstract) elicits a new mixture of images. They are reinforced by the explicit removal of *all* aversions ("I will fear no evil").

Although these periods of self-comfort are produced merely by placing old words in new orders, they are associated with the experiences of insight and quiet understanding. You can tell their effects. The faces of the audience abound with open mouths, smiles of inspiration, and the wide eyes of sudden enlightenment.

Metaphors, like poetry, about God concepts must be vague. If any component can be translated into a real and testable situation, the effectiveness is lost. It's a little like the disappointment when you meet, on a one-to-one basis, a well-known personage. Somehow they're not as tall or as good-looking.

Successful and popular religious speakers manipulate metaphors. The effective priest, minister, or shaman speaks of "souls dangling over the pits of hell," of scientists who are "children trying to spell God with the wrong blocks," or the "lamb of God" as "the spring of eternal salvation."

To appreciate the role of metaphors in religious semantics, read a transcript of an inspiring sermon and then compare it with the listening experience. There is a large difference. The same phrases that included enlightenment appear trivial and sometimes even ludicrous.

The actual test for the prediction that God words and God language are anxiety reducers for the semantic self is clear. If God words are maintained by their consequences (anxiety reduction), then they should occur most frequently during times and in situations of anxiety production.

Environmental uncertainty is a major source of anxiety. Floods, hurricanes, tornadoes, and earthquakes are historical sources. Cultures that have been faced with these unpredictable disasters have many God words. Today, hurricanes (and to some extent flooding) are no longer sources of unpredictability; they are almost totally foreseeable. On the other hand, earthquakes are still, for the moment, outside the realm of day-to-day prediction. Since earthquakes are common sources of death and cultural disruption, they are still paired with God words.

Human behavior is still another source of anxiety. "Wars and rumors of wars," to borrow a quote from a popular testament, always exist. Although the locus of the anticipation may change from Iran to Poland or from Germany to Japan, the anticipation is still an anxiety source.

People are unaware of the recurrent nature of human conflict. Each generation, which can never directly experience the beliefs of its predecessors, is convinced that present crises are more important. The past has occurred, and consequently there is no anxiety there.

To further test the variables that control the use of God words, we would have to construct a life anxiety scale. This measure would be a cumulative index of the number of negative stimuli that are anticipated for the future. The greater the percentge of negative stimuli composing the average person's daily life, the more likely God words will be expressed.

Today, in the 1980s, like the many cycles that have waxed and waned before us, this generation has been exposed to an imminent feeling of negative anticipation. It arises from many sources, including economic hardship, political unrest throughout the world, and even the unprecedented eruption of Mount St. Helens. It is nurtured by the evening news, when the deterioration of big cities and the disintegration of the nation's moral fabric are reported with the price of pork. It is encouraged by the buried expectations of 1984 and the obsession-compulsion for the year 2000. It is fostered by the reflex-like consensus that the outbreak of World War III is just a matter of time.

God words and God beliefs are expected features of contemporary anxiety. From any clinical perspective, they are healthy rituals that keep anxiety at bay. The danger arises when people begin to believe that God words are just as real as a nuclear explosion. Sticks and stones may break your bones, but atomic bombs will kill you.

8

Techniques for Integrating Religious Behaviors: From Rituals to Revelation

God is the single most powerful human experience. Because of the intense sense of meaningfulness and conviction associated with it, the God Belief defies routine rational analysis. Because of the conditioned connection between God concepts and the sense of self, the episode is difficult to deny.

Human beings have tortured themselves and countless animals in order to obtain access to God associations. Men from one subculture have killed men from another in order to test whose verbal sequences were correct—Allah is great, or is God even better?

Considering the prevalence and persistence of God Experiences among the human species, the evolution of social organizations that feed on these episodes is expected. These social structures have been called "religious organizations" or, more simply, "religions." They involve symbols, places, people, and procedures.

Large numbers of responses are generated around basic biological events. The more important events, those that are immediately relevant to the survival of the organism, are associated with the most extensive physiological changes. They are also associated with the most complex behavioral patterns.

Human beings are characterized by their versatility of response to the same thing. For the simple act of reproduction, most cultures have generated hundreds of specific behavioral patterns that must be displayed. They include meeting, dating, marrying, and engaging in the intrinsic biological reinforcer of sex. However, even this response can only be performed in particular ways.

For the simple consumptive sequences called "eating," human cultures have developed a variety of expected patterns. Food must be prepared in specific ways. Only certain kinds of foods must be eaten while others must be avoided.

One cannot eat with one's fingers (which is just as effective as a fork), but must dine with cutlery.

Still further rituals are applied to the innate tendency to kill. A member of any human group cannot kill another member of his or her group without suffering harsh consequences. However, if he or she kills a member of another group during an organized slaughter, he or she receives a medal and clear rewards.

The God Experience, although traditionally not treated as a biologically based phenomenon, has generated similar group behaviors. There are special sequences for obtaining God effects. There are special places or conditions in which they must occur.

Religious organizations are powerful social forces. People within these organizations, whether they are popes, priests, witch doctors, or shamans, control and focus the manner in which God Experiences occur. They influence, even dictate, the interpretation in which the experiences are cast.

Organized religions are more than the people who maintain the rituals. Religions are semantic reinforcement schedules that structure the environment. They contain explanations for why adversity must happen (why negative stimuli are presented). They outline the responses that must be displayed in order to obtain rewards.

Because all human beings contain the biological propensity and the early childhood conditioning to make them susceptible to God Experiences, religious organizations (and the people in power) maintain an impressive control over human populations. As long as human beings experience cosmic meaning and play semantic games, the massive Christian and Islamic organizations (to name two communities) will continue to win converts.

The success of religions is totally dependent on their pervasiveness and persistence in everyday life. Rituals and rhythms are so interwoven within a person's reinforcement (reward-punishment) history that they become a part of his or her personality. This principle is clearly evident in the religious indoctrination of children.

Well-established organizations, like Catholic, Islamic, Protestant, or Jewish groups, pair the tenets of religion with prayers or contemplations during school, initiation rites into adulthood (confirmation, bar mitzvah, baptisms) and intervals of reward (holidays, gift giving).

Aspiring cults have employed similar methods of entrenchment. For example, the Transcendental Meditation Organization has attempted a grass-roots approach by sponsoring good neighbor medals, outstanding citizen awards, athletic competitions, and even activities in the grammar school classroom (Persinger, Carrey, and Suess 1980). They have been less successful than orthodox religions; competition is tough, especially between religions.

Religions contain rules that serve both to reinforce the God concept and to maintain the person's dedication to the organization. One version of a popular rule is, "honor thy father and thy mother." This practice, if followed rigorously, is easily generalized to "Honor the parent surrogate," the God Concept.

Explanations for adversity are common options given by religions. Many foster paranoid themes by rationalizing real or imagined persecution. If a person is taught, "People do bad things to me because I am a Jew," then every time something negative occurs (regardless of the reason), the person concludes, "It was because I am a Jew." As a result, the number of pairings with the person's concept of himself or herself and the associations of Jew are strengthened. The explanation gives structure to the nuances of human behaviors. It actively maintains the associations of the religion.

However, all religions are counterfeit organizations of explanation, dictate, and ritual. Churches, synagogues, and mosques are completely irrelevant to the God Experience. The Bible, Koran, and Book of the Dead are pages of absolute nonsense. They contain arbitrary value judgments masked in poetry and generalities. These neutral stimuli become important because they are associated with the person's temporal lobe displays.

The techniques by which religious organizations develop personal significance and cultural relevance involve several kinds of conditioning. Unlike more mundane behaviors, religious concepts pervade the culture. To be most effective, they are paired at all levels of human behavior.

The first stage, the specific conditioning of the characteristics of the God concept, is completed by pairing it with essential biological activities. God words like *Jehovah*, *Allah*, *Yahweh*, or *the Great Spirit* are paired with eating, sleeping, and the general delivery of positive things.

As I have mentioned in previous chapters, the most optimal conditioning for brief responses (like eating) occurs when the neutral (and initially irrelevant) stimulus is presented *before* the primary or biological reinforcer. Once the pairing has occurred, the neutral stimulus can be called a conditioned stimulus, since it elicits responses similar to those produced by the biological reinforcer.

God words presented before eating are optimally conditioned. Prayers such as "God is great, God is good, now we thank Him for our food" are reinforced by the presentation and consumption of the food. After a few pairings, the prayers begin to elicit expectations of warmth, satisfaction, and biologically rewarding experiences.

The pairing becomes involuntary; it becomes a ritual. By the time a person from a religious family is 15 years of age, he has paired prayer with eating about *ten thousand times*. The number of presentations determines the intensity of the learning.

Can you imagine the significance of any word that has been paired ten thousand times with something as important as eating? Even the most nonsensical phrase would become a potent conditioned stimulus. Later, when it was presented alone, it would elicit all kinds of positive and pleasant sensations.

God words are also acquired as explanations for unanswered questions or for periods of adversity and personal dilemma. Religions contain suggestions or instructions to "ask God" when all else fails. One such popular phrase is, "Ask and you will receive; seek and you will find."

Unfortunately, they are also taught as "solutions" (which they are not) to complex problems. The situation is similar to the manner in which children are taught to feel inferior or stupid. If a child spills a glass of milk, a typical response is to berate the child for his clumsiness. With enough of these associations, the child begins to call himself the same words. Worst of all, he begins to respond as if he were incompetent.

The more appropriate conditioning in this episode would be to say, "All right, you've spilled the milk, now get a cloth and clean it up." Through the pairing of the problem (the spilt milk) with a clear solution (cleaning it up with a cloth), the child has been given a procedure instead of a deleterious label that could influence his personality and punish his ability to solve problems objectively.

Religious organizations foster the former type of response. Instead of attempting to solve the problem by rational procedures, the person is taught to pray or ask God. Essentially, the message is this: you, as an individual, are incompetent because you cannot solve the problem, hence you give up and ask a parent surrogate. The only access to the God parent surrogate is only through a particular religious organization. (Otherwise, why not pray to other deities like Zeus or the Great Kahuna instead of Allah or God?)

A second stage by which religious symbols and dogma are weaved into a society involves persistent pairing with key biological events. The most significant landmarks are births, sanctions for sexual behavior (marriage), and death. These three stimuli are notorious sources of biological and behavioral stimulation. They are shared in some way by every human being.

By localizing the occurrence of biological events within churches, synagogues, mosques, and special regions of the land, these areas have been paired with primary rewards. By pairing religious words of the Bible, Koran, or local bard with biological necessities, meaningless phrases have achieved significance.

To appreciate the importance of this learning, consider, if you have been trained as a Christian, how "nonsensical" 100,000 Islamic worshippers look as they assume the fetal position on some straw mats. Yet, the sounds of a Gregorian chant or the voices of the Sunday choir can induce a deep sense of significance.

However, if you are an Islamic believer, you might wonder how those infidels could sing among themselves to some Jewish God whose alleged people spurn them as Gentiles. You would only find meaning in the mourning chant of the seer and the prostrate position of respectful submission.

The supreme irony of this entire conditioning pattern is that churches, scriptures, and the people who maintain them are irrelevant to the biological behaviors. Without the consistent pairing of religious behaviors with those fundamental reinforcers, organized religion would be only another form of entertainment and diversion.

Perhaps one of the easiest ways to understand how religious organizations and symbols can attain personal significance is to analyze missionary procedures. Missionaries can be defined as people who attempt: (1) to modify or extinguish the God concepts of people from other cultures and (2) to shape or condition the God concepts from their own.

The most fundamental principle of missionary operations is the pairing of new ideas, new verbal sequences, with fundamental biological requirements. Since most cultures already contain God words and religious organizations, the biological requirement must be quite substantial.

One of the most effective biological reinforcers has been food. In order to use food reinforcement as a reward for learning new material, the human beings must be food deprived. Since starvation has been an extraordinarily common event among both Western and non-Western cultures, conditioning has not been difficult.

Shaping is done slowly and gradually. At first, the local people are required to listen to the stories about God, Christ, Allah, or Yahweh. These new verbal sequences are associated with or followed by food. A similar procedure is used in Protestant Sunday schools and Bible schools, where the stories are followed by "refreshments." A more honest description would be the responses (themselves meaningless) are followed by food rewards.

As the person learns the stories, she obtains more food or greater access to special privileges. The individual is rewarded for repetition or imitation of the stories. Various applications, such as, "Is my persecution by the tribe similar to the persecution of the Christians by the Romans?" are rewarded by smiles, acknowledgments, and increased access to psychological rewards.

These techniques have worked very well in cultures where people were routinely exposed to food or water deprivations. Any series of behaviors, no matter how nonsensical, can become conditioned stimuli if they are paired with the removal of hunger.

For these individuals, the new God words are associated with feelings of comfort, satiation, and joy. Since God stories have been paired so many times with the consequent removal of hunger, the stories generate a similar psychological experience.

If the conditioning is strong enough, just thinking about God concepts can produce anticipations of food delivery. When food is finally delivered, the concept is reinforced. If the food is not delivered, the person dies, and is unable to challenge what has been taught.

When the individual can generate more than just a rote repetition of what he has been told about the new God concepts, he is considered a convert. The ability to generate new applications of the God concept to the person's life and to the world around him is called *response generalization*. It indicates that he has acquired the task.

Acquisition of the new material is evident when the person uses sentences like "I am a Christian" or "I am a follower of Islam." The demonstration that the semantic self has been paired with the new ideas is measured by the frequency of their occurrence and the pervasiveness of their display in the person's life style.

Once the symbol system has been clearly established and the God words have been strongly conditioned, further reinforcements are made contingent on still further behaviors. The new convert must attend church and contribute a part of his production (earnings, farm produce, or time) to benefit the religious group.

Semantic components of the religious organization become more important. This "indoctrination" involves the acquisition of a sophisticated series of words to explain why you will die (and where you will go) and how to live every day.

Words and word sequences become reinforcing by themselves. The new convert spends time repeating phrases like "Go ye therefore into the world and teach all nations" or "Whatever is in the heavens and whatever is in the earth, proclaims the Holiness of God. He is the first and He is the last, and the Manifest and the Hidden" (from the Koran). These become sources of stimulation, especially when reinforced by smiles, words of encouragement, and comradery.

An important function of any religious organization is to recruit other members. It may be legitimized by a variety of compatible arguments. One organization may argue that conversion or recruitment is the best means of saving lost souls. Another organization may argue that people are not human beings unless they are converted (and hence can be killed or enslaved).

Recruitment is critical because it maintains the religious organization. One does not require a conspiracy hypothesis that some group of people is secretly pulling strings to stimulate converts. Instead, the more people who are converted, the more people repeat the themes of the organization and hence the more people are converted. The growth is no more mysterious than cell division in a culture of bacteria.

The primate tendency to *imitate* sources of reward is important in the recruitment process. Whereas children tend to imitate the parent who is most associated with reward-punishment, the depressed and anxious person is more likely to imitate a person whose behavior suggests reduction of this negative condition. There is little more suggestive than a smiling, euphoric, dynamic person who effervesces with purpose and assurance.

The private conversation of the potential convert goes something like this: "I am depressed and confused; this smiling, dynamic person is not. He is not because he believes in God. Consequently, if I imitate this behavior, I, too, will feel that way." This behavior is not uncommon; it lies at the basis of getting hairdos that make you look like movie stars or adopting the habits of a favorite person.

Missionary operations may utilize biological essentials other than food as the first step in the conditioning process. In addition to food, medical treatment has been very popular. Medical treatment means the removal of pain and aversion due to disease and illness. Any response that is followed by the removal of aversive stimuli is rewarded.

Religious organizations proliferate in and around areas of relief from sickness, such as hospitals or drug dispensaries. By simply pairing the new God concept with the reduction of pain and recovery from illness, the new words are clearly rewarded. Of course, religious explanations and the presence of crosses, candles, priests, ministers, or holy men have absolutely nothing to do with the survival of the patient. The reason that people are not dying now from most diseases but were dying one hundred years ago has nothing to do with religion; it hasn't changed. What has changed is the medical technology.

The ability of missionaries to manipulate the essential biological factors of nutrition and health has been a central source of their success. Since religions have been invariably associated with environmental events that people can control least, words paired with the control of these events are directly associated with God concepts.

After all, suppose you were a member of a culture that lived from year to year on a subsistence level. In order to explain this uncertainty, you say the delivery of food and the occurrence of disease are due to "spirits." When they are happy, there is ample food; when they are not, then you starve.

Because of the illusion of the egocentric reference, you blame yourself or, more likely, some poor scapegoat for the adversity. Your technology does not allow you to see that ample food is tightly coupled to the cycles of the weather. Your science does not indicate that famine would be predictable if you had the appropriate knowledge.

Then along comes an odd person who talks about an invisible force floating around the sky. Even though it sounds nonsensical, these people appear to control what you cannot. They are sources of inexhaustible food supplies and they can cure diseases which until this time were deadly. The connection between the God concept and the new arrivals would not require much active reasoning.

There is little doubt that enhanced technology and the relative lack of deprivation were responsible for the failure of foreign religions to proliferate in the West. If you were a comfortable nineteenth century person who had ample food and fair medical aid, would you be impressed with a God concept that was paired with the small of bark broth, and two sweet potatoes in a basket?

Positive rewards are optimal consequences for conditioning new God words. But there are two other conditioning paradigms. Both are associated with delivery of negative stimuli (or punishments). They differ in that one is associated with the removal of the aversive experiences, whereas the other is associated with their presentation.

The first option requires that some natural catastrophe occur, such as an earthquake, flood, tornado, or hurricane. It is best to have a natural catastrophe that is commonly paired with the local God concepts. Classic procedures are to distribute food, blankets, and sources of shelter after the natural cataclysm. Catholic missionaries have developed this technique well. Each time they pass out a blanket or serve some corn, rice, or milk, the association between the particular God concept and survival becomes strengthened.

Singular major catastrophes are more impressive than daily traumas. The former induce a more drastic and widespread privation, the relief from which produces maximum reward. Under such duress, only a single pairing of a God concept with the removal of the privation can maintain the connection for a lifetime.

The second alternative to positive reward is simple avoidance of punishment. Stated in everyday words, this type of recruitment goes like this: "I have a religion; if you do not believe the same way, I will kill you." As you might suspect, this approach produces quick consequences.

There are a couple of drawbacks to this type of God conditioning. In the first place, the anticipation of punishment induces much anxiety within the society. Anticipation of being killed or losing a hand because you don't say the appropriate God words can be quite disruptive. The Islamic religion uses it now, but the Catholics have used it before through threats of excommunication. This approach produces a general reduction of behaviors other than just alternative religious ideas. Creativity is suppressed and individuality is removed. There is a great deal of stereotype and imitation (placating) within this framework.

The second major limit of this approach is its relatively quick extinction. As long as the punishment is maintained, the God concept is revered. However, as soon as the punishment is removed, and not just replaced with another punisher, the behaviors are no longer displayed. Instead, there is a brief period of nonspecific and flurried response (anarchy).

Once the basic conditioning to the God concept has occurred, religious organizations must maintain the behavior. Over the years, religious organizations in all cultures have developed similar patterns. Considering the dependence of religion on basic human behaviors, these similarities are no more surprising than the observation that people in all human cultures walk on two legs.

Four major control variables are apparent in religious organizations. They include: the emphasis on the *egocentric reference*, the selection of a *particular space*, the incorporation of *rituals*, and the significance of certain *verbal sequences*. Each of these maintains and strengthens the persistence of the religion.

All religions encourage feelings of individual uniqueness. Since the basic source of religious behaviors is individual experience, the necessity for this activity is evident. As mentioned in Chapter 4, the power of the proof is almost totally contingent upon personal experience.

Either by design or by consequence, proponents of most religious organizations realize that few people will indict their own experiences. To challenge or doubt one's own experience is to doubt one's concept of self. The anxiety and uncertainty are just too intense.

Religious organizations feed on this tendency by asking the person to judge for himself or herself. Although it presents the guise of a free choice, the request is clearly lopsided before it is asked. Few people are going to say, "God talked to me but there is also a statistical likelihood that it was a quirk of my brain."

Although religions control the external reinforcement schedules (means to rewards), responses to them must be maintained in order to keep the person within the confines of the group. External schedules shape shared group experiences and increased solidarity.

However, some allowance must be made for personal access. Personal access to God associations allows direct reinforcement (it's like a child getting as close as possible to its mother). The person can pray to God without going through an indirect and less rewarding route, such as a priest, minister, or holy man. Predictably, the belief in a personal God has had great appeal in many cultures. This custom-made superparent concept can be accessed at any time and anywhere.

The history of religious movements can be seen within this context. New religions, even contemporary ones, emerge when church rewards have been slowly removed from quick access. There have been times in the history of humanity when gaining such rewards was a pretty chancy business. These periods heralded reformations (Adler, 1972).

The second major control variable of religious organizations is the importance of a place in which to display religious behaviors. The locus may be called a church, mosque, synagogue, kingdom hall, holy place, or mana region. It contains three important properties: *unique associations*, features that induce *diminutive experiences*, and the *close proximity of people*.

Unique associations are critical for producing the potency of the effect. This is created by pairing only (or primarily) religious behaviors with the place. As a result, the place itself becomes a cue (a discriminative stimulus) for inducing all types of religious behaviors.

Unique associations are responsible for the success of many "pure" experiences. The success of mantras (sounds repeated during meditation), for example, is due to their nonsense and novelty. Because there are no previous associations with these sounds, the new response (relaxation) can more easily be paired with them.

As many experiments have shown, just about any word can be used as a mantra. However, everyday words have competing associations. You could use the word *turkey* as a mantra. But this word is contaminated by associations with the country, the bird, and your next-door neighbor.

As long as reverent, respectful, and God-related behaviors are associated with churches and synagogues, they are primary foci for the occurrence of these responses. The buildings lose their effectiveness as discriminative stimuli when they become paired with mundane and casual behaviors such as watching television, playing games, or sleeping.

Features that induce diminutive experiences are important for fostering the sensations of dependence and helplessness, important components of the God Experience. This experience is conditioned from the periods of infancy, when the child's visual field is filled with the faces of its parents.

Diminutive experiences in the adult can be induced in any perceptual context where the ground is very much larger than the figure (the person). Extraordinarily large buildings (cathedrals) produce impressive diminutive effects. They were, however, more commanding stimuli before the days of giant skyscrapers and massive cities.

Natural structures are also perceptually effective for inducing diminutive experiences. Mountains, against which the person appears trivial, and deserts, within which the person is minuscule, are excellent stimuli for precipitating God Experiences. So-called breathtaking perceptions, another way of saying "the stimuli flood the perceptual system," such as brilliant sunsets or views from the tops of mountains, are candidates. In the later case, hypoxia certainly helps.

Group gatherings are also facilitated in "holy" places. Frankly, there are many phenomena associated with the close proximity of many human beings (groups) that are not well understood. The dynamics of mob behavior is only one example.

One primary feature is the enhanced frequency of touching. Touch is an important experience in human life; it is the first sensation by which we perceive the world. The sense of touch is paired with intimacy, trust, general dependence, and security. Touch is also a powerful stimulus that can unleash behaviors that have not been shown since infancy. A common response when close touching is allowed in adult groups is the display of tears and cries for the parent. They are followed by a sense of having a burden lifted and a greater solidarity with the group. Religious organizations are some of the few institutions in the Western world in which touch is still tolerated. "Laying on of hands," "group retreats," and "fellowship meetings" are common terms for bouts of close touching. Crying and confessions are not uncommon.

There are other group behaviors that are now found primarily in the context of religious organizations. One of the most common shared experiences is singing in groups. The times of people singing together as they followed the bouncing ball on the movie screen are gone. So is that sense of group cohesion. Sounds and songs are significant precipitators of the God Experience (just note the number of sudden conversions during the final hymn of a Billy Graham crusade). When sung in a group, routine music can induce bouts of sobbing and weeping.

When the entire group is activated, a mob-like psychology appears. At the peak of the group arousal, the members are convinced they are right. Subtle cues are taken as proof of their conviction; there is no rational counterargument. The panics on Wall Street and communist scares should have taught us that.

Within the group, religious experiences obtain a special flavor. Since everyone's brain is stimulated, even the most nonsensical events become meaningful. It is like a group déjà vu experience where something that has not been seen or heard before is experienced as familiar.

Some episodes of "speaking in tongues," which is an overinclusive label for many different phenomena, show this effect. As the amount of brain stimulation increases and the dissociation begins, basic sounds are emitted. Most of them are elementary composites of what the person has heard (or thinks are the sounds of Hebrew, for example). Since the lower parts of the brain are still functioning, the sounds are still integrated phonemes, although the sequences are meaningless.

The members of the group, all aroused by the intensity of the songs, music, and previous associations, assume that the shared meaningfulness is due to a "spirit" that permeates the group. They do not realize that the meaningfulness originates with neither the words nor the "spirit," but from their individual brains. The phenomenon is the modification of experience and not a spiritual manifestation.

They are no more "in the spirit" than a group of people drinking in the same tavern. The experience is no more real than groups of Chinese "infested by the monkey god" or Haitian voodoo dancers "possessed by spirits." The similarities lie in the environmental pattern that precipitates the experience and in the fundamental construction of the human brain.

Everything, animate or inanimate, displays certain properties related to its construction. A property of round rocks is to roll down hillsides. A property of suspension bridges is to fall apart, literally, following the appropriate vibrations. A property of human bone is to generate electric currents when it is deformed. One of the most common built-in properties of human behavior is the maintenance of certain behaviors that are irrelevant to the delivery of any clear rewards. They comprise the third major control variable of religious organizations: rituals. Rituals are repeated sequences of responses that can range from moving hands across the head and heart to pointing an erect penis in the direction of an adversary.

Rituals are maintained because of what does *not* happen. The failure for adversity to occur is the primary fuel for rituals. They are maintained because adverse events are much less frequent than the number of times most rituals can be completed.

If every time a sequence of responses occurred, punishment followed, the responses would be quickly repressed. However, by chance alone, there must be certain responses, in every human culture, that occur but which are not always punished. The longer the period before some punishment occurs, the more effectively these responses are rewarded.

One ritual would be repeating the phrase "God protect us from harm." In this instance, the assumption is that God can shelter the person from harm. If harm is relatively infrequent, the ritual will rarely be punished. In fact, the majority of times the person says the prayer, no harm follows. The fact that no harm would follow anyway, no matter what the person said, is not realized. The critical operation is that the statement was made and no adversity followed. Privately, the person concludes that the ritual was the reason the adversity was avoided.

It's an interesting semantic circle whose full implications can be seen in a more secular example. One day in New York City, there was a man on a bus who was shredding up pieces of paper and throwing them out the window. The bus driver watched him carefully, suspecting that the man was some kind of nut. After several hours of this behavior, the driver could wait no longer. He went to the back of the bus and asked the man why he was shredding the paper. The man replied, "To keep away the wild tigers." The driver exclaimed, "But there are no tigers in New York City." The man replied, "See, it works!"

Religious rituals follow a similar logic. They are maintained when adversities happen infrequently. If the prayers say, "protect us from starvation" and starvation is infrequent, or "protect us from death" and death is infrequent, then every time the prayer is said and no adversity follows, the ritual is reinforced.

Considering this mechanism, it is easy to see why the most effective rituals are usually displayed daily, or at most weekly. Since major adverse events generally occur only between intervals of years, hundreds of these rituals are followed by *no* adversity, pain, or punishment.

When occasional adversity does occur, despite the ritual, the importance of those hundreds of "avoidances" becomes evident. The death of a family member, even immediately after you prayed for safety, punishes only that *one* response. The adversity does not affect the positive effects of the hundreds of other responses.

Once the ritual is established, the sequence becomes a source of structure and familiarity in the environment. Deviations from this habit induce uncertainty, and this is followed by uneasiness. Another word for that uneasiness is *anxiety*. This experience of anxiety is familiar to anyone who has "forgotten" to say prayers before bedtime or to repeat the dinner grace. The failure to display the response is followed by anxiety. However, by saying the prayers, the anxiety is reduced and consequently the prayers are even more reinforced.

The same experience can be induced by breaking any habit. The reader may try this test to demonstrate the point. Hang a copy of President Reagan near an accessible spot in your office or kitchen. Every time you pass the photograph, smile, salute, and tap him on the head. After three continuous weeks of this behavior (three times a day), take the picture down. For the first few days, you'll feel a sense of uneasiness, as if you have forgotten something. It has more to do with ritual than with Reagan.

Since rituals are primarily maintained by the failure of anxiety or adversity to follow, cultures that contain a larger percentage of drought, pain, hunger, and unexpected negative stimuli should have more daily rituals than cultures living in a more comfortable environment. These cultures should have a greater portion of their daily lives oriented toward the exact sequence of religious rituals. Anthropologists have repeatedly confirmed these observations.

Within Western culture, the durations of daily ritual time appear to be directly related to the daily levels of uncertainty. Not surprisingly, the number of Hail Marys increases markedly during international crises. The repetitions of "Allah Akhbar!" are most numerous when the future is uncertain and war looms on the horizon.

There is always great individual variation to God references; this reflects the learning patterns of the person. If the individual had been always rewarded for believing in the omnipotence of God because the environment was replete with rewards (food, warmth, and bicycles), the sudden loss, for the first time, of a parent, spouse, or close friend could produce a kind of frustrative aggression. It would be directed against the alleged source of the rewards: God. He or She would be considered worthless.

On the other hand, if the delivery of rewards, such as food and sex, and the occurrence of bad events were more intermittent (a more usual condition), then God extinction would be less likely. The *variable interval schedule* of rewards (or escape from negative events) is notorious for maintaining behaviors over extended periods. It's the same powerful schedule that maintains the compulsive gambler—sooner or later something has to occur, and by chance alone it does.

Special word sequences compose the fourth control variable of any religious organization. Two types of word sequences are important: God words and magic or secret words. Both are used sparingly and in specific contexts. Believers cannot use God words in any situation that eliminates the effectiveness of the associations. Since habituation (that is, frequent repetition of any response) eliminates its rewarding aspects, a common taboo is "Thou shalt not take the name of the Lord thy God in vain." The potency and arousal properties of any word, even a curse, are lost if it is repeated frequently enough.

A second prohibition is the pairing of God words with conditions that erode the presumption of omnipotence and respect. Consequently, most God words cannot be used in contexts of mockery or fun. Such pairings would contaminate the associations with God words. They would lose their effectiveness.

Magic words are also important in a religious organization. They control the person's behavior, since the acquisition of the words is made dependent on the display of appropriate behaviors. They may include attending church, keeping the faith, or committing some unlawful act.

Like mantras, the most effective religious words are new or meaningless to initiates. With no previous associations, only the religious symbols are paired to the new phrases. They become intense and reliable cues for controlling religious behaviors.

To non-Latin speakers, the Catholic Mass in Latin functioned in a mantra-like manner. Since the language was meaningless to the listener, except in a direct association with religious concepts, the language became a powerful trigger for unleashing those experiences. The sudden removal of Latin from the Mass was a strong disruptive source for these previous associations. People who had been dependent on Latin cues for their experiences began looking for other substitutes. One solution was the substitution of Latin with another series of nonsense phrases, such as "speaking in tongues."

Modern quasi-religions have utilized other languages as sources of verbal rituals. Asian and Middle Eastern languages, such as Sanskrit or (allegedly) ancient Egyptian (Budge 1967) are most popular since they have been paired with the mystique of ancient power and profound understanding. Although the words and phrases are meaningless to the initiate, the connotations contribute to expectations.

Verbal sequences are usually acquired in steps. The person must progress through stages of initiation or enlightenment in order to obtain more rewards. However, there is always a catch to this system. There are built-in limits—one can never obtain all the steps.

In the Christian religion, for example, the various steps involve committing fewer and fewer sins. The end point is some stage of perfection or Christ-like characteristic. However, this can never really be obtained, if one reads the small print, because everyone is imperfect by definition.

The existence of verbal steps ensures that people will spend a lifetime engaging in the behaviors that make them dependent on the religious organization. It is much like the belt system in the martial arts. Although one can learn to fight relatively quickly, a step system fosters associations with the people and practices of the system.

Considering the intimate relationship between anxiety reduction and the God Concept, religious organizations can be expected to flourish in human groups plagued by uncertainty, deprivation, and primitive science. Even a crude analysis of the last 2,000 years of history demonstrates that relationship.

Christianity itself emerged among peoples who were faced with daily privation and trauma, and who had a long history of pain. If old historical records can be taken at face value, most of the early converts were either slaves or people who lived in the mire of poverty. Is it any wonder that the promises of golden streets, eternal life, and a land of milk and honey were attractive? What did these people have to lose when they had nothing? In times of torment, even the most far-fetched ideas acquire a glimmer of possibility.

If you add the pairing of God Concepts with food and drink (like the body–bread and wine–blood metaphors), the security and comradery of the group, the comfort of daily ritual, and the essential stroking of individual uniqueness (through the belief that not even a sparrow is overlooked), the attraction can be overpowering.

It is also obvious why people who had a history of working and receiving rewards, such as bankers and tradesmen, were less impressed by these words.

Why should one give up the goods for which one has worked for a handful of promises? When a person's decision is a matter of the specific learning history, the truth of any universal message becomes suspect.

Contemporary religious organizations still spread best in areas of deprivation and hopelessness. Christianity grows strongest in low socioeconomic classes that have had long histories of meager living combined with occasional rewards. It is still more easily maintained in populations repressed by poor education and the smothering persistence of tradition.

Islamic concepts have also proliferated in similar environments. They have flowered in social climates where the majority of the people have had nothing. Islamic organizations have gathered strength in cultures where anxiety-producing innovations have threatened tradition.

Religious organizations also thrive during periods of anxiety and conflict. The old cliché that there is no atheist in a foxhole is most frequently said when the pews are full. This is forgotten when the conflict is over.

Until recently, religious organizations were nourished by one unchanging fact: The future is unpredictable. When the Western world was full of daily starvation, death, and little hope, religious organizations dominated humanity. They exhibited extraordinary political power. But as the world became more predictable, their power faded. As the unknowns of this planet were described, food access in the Northern Hemisphere became routine, and many diseases were eliminated, religious organizations were no longer useful. Their last pocket of persistence was the most fearful unknown of them all: personal death.

Now, religious organizations only occasionally dominate. There are always unpredicted natural disaster and rumors of war. These occasional injections of environmental uncertainty can initiate, almost overnight, an epidemic of revival.

9
The Religious Personality

Is there a religious personality? Are there some people who are more prone to having religious experiences than others? These two critical and complex questions will be answered in this chapter. However, we have already learned about the types of response profiles that would characterize religious behaviors. Since personality is primarily a consequence of the learning patterns to which the person has been exposed, certain types of reinforcement histories are expected to generate religious behaviors. They would be encouraged by early paradigms of superstitious conditioning and excessive parental dependence.

There is also the transient component: the God Experience. Although religious beliefs are highly correlated with the occurrence of these transients, there are discrepancies. A person who has been conditioned by parental reinforcement and peer group pressure to believe in God may never have had a God Experience. Similarly, a person may have many God Experiences but not follow any accepted religious belief. Multiple close communions with the Creator would be difficult to maintain within the rigid ritual of an orthodox order. Instead, these people pursue a more mystical philosophy (Clark 1958).

As noted in the first two chapters, God Experiences are distributed along a temporal lobe continuum. It is dominated by the stability of specific nuclei deep in the human brain. God Experiences, in this context, occur as small microseizures within the temporal lobe; they are triggered by the chemical consequences of personal stress, hypoglycemia, fatigue, hypoxia, anxiety, and a variety of idiosyncratic neurophysiological anomalies. Learning patterns and reinforcement history both complement and extend temporal lobe structure and function.

These conditions allow for the coherence of the deep structures (within the temporal lobe) that are typically not correlated at all. This is an important condition, since God Experiences, in the normal population, are transient events invariably triggered by some form of biochemical crises. In populations prone to repeated microseizures and more frequent coherence between typically uncorrelated structures, religious-type experiences are almost a daily occurrence. Such individuals, who comprise a clinical subpopulation of temporal lobe psychotics, are prone to multiple conversions and daily communion with deities.

The critical feature is the coherence among portions of the human temporal lobe that are usually separated by incompatible electrical frequencies or simple neuronal circuitry. When the coherence occurs, these portions of the brain blend together into a functional whole or unit. Experiences correlated with these divided structures combine to form new collages of images and sensations. If they include a cluster of reward nuclei (groups of neurons whose primary experiential correlate is that of intense pleasure or positive affect), then the images will be remembered in detail, and their meaning will seem profound.

Occasionally, aversive nuclei would be involved. Correlative experiences are saturated by intense sensations of pain and intolerable negative emotions. Images paired with these gut emotions flood the person's awareness. From this source arises the expectation of hell. The pain of fire, the smell of sulfur, and the terror of eternal damnation are temporal lobe themes displayed in religious dogma. For the most part, such experiences would suppress any further displays. The person just would not remember the events, although an inkling of apprehension may be associated with a blank memory. However, considering the hundreds of thousands of positive experiences, there must be occasional episodes where hell is "experienced" and remembered.

When the coherence occurs, old memories, long isolated by the processes of maturation, are revived. Twilight images last experienced a billion seconds before and now hidden within a myriad array of dendritic patterns, become accessible. Old images of parental power blend with contemporary concepts of abstract gods in time and space. Pure affect, last felt during periods of absolute dependence and complete satiation within the crib, combine with feelings of cosmic meaning. The potent affect of the child converges with the intellect of the adult thinker. The limits of infantile perceptions expand to the universe's edge and the God-parent waits, somewhere, to bring intellectual warmth and to remove the anxiety of existence.

These nuclei of the brain contain the experiential correlates of space-time; when they are stimulated, even by crude electrodes, people experience alterations in time. It appears to speed up or to slow down. When these portions of the brain are excited, space changes. Objects are seen in different contexts. People feel as if they are somewhere else. Their bodies are there, but "they" are somewhere else. There are a variety of words applied to these experiences; they are called "depersonalization" in the laboratory and "astral projection" by those who prefer a more mystical interpretation.

The affective sense of self is stimulated in the temporal lobe as well. It is made evident by the experience of being "more than one person" when these parts of the brain are stimulated. The evidence is clear when the person feels that the "real" self has separated from the body. Whereas the body image, composed of the numerous sensory inputs from along the skin and within the muscles, may be the ultimate source of these experiences, the sense of self can seem to occur quite independently of them. Occasionally, they are separated and the person feels himself or herself to be the pure and true entity, while the body is a separate thing.

No doubt the sense of self depends on ceaseless inputs from sensors throughout our body. When brief periods of desynchrony occur and the deep structures of the temporal lobe and cortical portions of the parietal region become coherent, our sense of self does not suddenly change. We do not perceive ourselves as another person, but as the same entity who for a brief moment has mingled with the cosmic consciousness; many label it as God. Only when more pathological (and discernable) processes are involved does a person see himself or herself as some nonhuman object.

Since the sense of self and of time and space are dominant within the same functional networks that contain old parental images and their symbolic extensions, intermingling of the God Concept and the sense of self is not surprising. The two are expected to be so intricately interrelated that one evokes the manifestation of the other. When one wonders about reality (the "real" me), questions about time and space and their end (death) are necessary concomitants. When thought sequences are generated about the diminutive self, alone in a terrifying infinity of eternal death, the sense of God emerges, shaped by the patterns of parental images.

During the temporal lobe transients that create the God Experience, body images of early infancy and childhood are transformed into adult formats. For a moment, the adult concepts of infinity and eternity are experienced with the emotions of the young child. Like the young child, whose universal boundary ends at the edges of his crib, the limits of space and time are blended with the sense of self. And somewhere outside the twilight boundaries of the cosmic crib, the parental surrogate waits to intervene. It is the most supreme form of egocentrism.

Beyond this limit, psychotic processes emerge. Whereas the normal individual, without psychiatric history, differentiates between the self and the God Concept, the psychotic confuses the two. They are merged together—God and the psychotic thinker become an identity; He or she *is* God. Comparable confusion can contaminate the normal God Experience, where, for the brief period of a TLT, the person may think he is a "son" or she is a "daughter" of God; they may even be God-like "things." However, the normal individual can return from the high and maintain the distinction. For a few wonderful seconds, he or she has mingled with God.

Considering the intricate connections between the sense of self and the God Concept, the confusion is not surprising. In fact, it is probably much more frequent than suspected, hidden from display by learned social consequences. The temporal lobe psychotic person, outside the institution, could indeed inhibit these convictions and maintain otherwise normal behaviors, but may believe that he is the son of God or she is another form of Mother Mary. The images would be fleeting, quickly accommodated and then repressed. A more secular variation could be the hunch or intuition that the person is "a child from an extragalactic super race" who is here to guide humanity.

The egocentrism of the God Experience is a predictable consequence of its shared neuronal sources. It cannot be impugned without indicting the sense of self. If the sense of self is questioned as an artifact of a long history of neuronal inputs derived from the chance convergence of one in a billion sperms with an egg, the anxiety of not being special emerges. If the sense of self falters, the omnipotence of God (or his space-time substitute of "cosmic consciousness" or the "infinite force") is questioned. As the self cracks, the terror of death and the unknown eat their way inward, and stark anxiety begins.

It is not surprising that those people who are most robustly religious should also be the most egocentric. By egocentric, then, we don't meant egotistical, arrogant, or narcissistic. Egocentrism means that the person places exaggerated emphasis, indeed supreme faith, in the validity of his or her experiences. The God episode is an extension. Although these people may appear open-minded and put on a display of objectivity (perhaps even with sincere intentions), their experiences are considered absolute. What they experience is real; there is no other possibility.

Egocentrism, then, is the first and paramount characteristic of the religious personality. Although they may be admirable individuals, who give themselves and their goods for the sake of the social good, their egocentrism prevails. They answer yes to questions such as, "I sincerely believe that I am a very special person" and "I have had a religious experience that I know was real." Privately, they perceive their behaviors as good or better than those of others, always with the repeated emphasis on the "I." The word may not be used, but the manner in which they display their behavior indicates their faith in their experiential validity.

It may take the form of the condescending believer who smiles with the wisdom of he who has a true glimpse into the universe, in response to questions about the validity of their God Experience. They cannot and will not challenge its validity; when they do, which is rare, the anxiety is incapacitating, and neurotic "breakdowns" are frequent. Instead, they smile and walk away, knowing that despite all other uncertainties that have ever been proven, only their experiences are true. There may even be the dress of great humility; it evokes public adoration. A most well-known example was Albert Einstein. He insisted on the minuscule importance of his creations, but when it came to his philosophical meandering, the egocentrism emerged: "I cannot believe that God plays dice with the universe."

It may take the form of the sincere converter, who, bubbling with conversion energy, wants to share her spiritual fortune with the world. Such a person may undergo economic hardship and cruel social derision in order to convince and to convert the people around her. She does not comprehend the egocentrism of the act. Why should her experience be somehow more real or valid than everyone else's? Why should one person's experience, no matter how personally profound, dominate all other people's existence?

When this form of egocentrism is rejected, the person develops a vindictive reaction to those who refuse to share. Others are seen as inhuman and lost forever. Since they do not share the same belief, they are just a little less human. So they can be manipulated or subjugated for "their own benefit." To the supreme shame of humanity, this manifestation of egocentrism has dominated the theme of missionary work. Catholics, Protestants, and Moslems have not differed in this.

It may take the form of the person who can measure all other things except his own experience against an objective scale. Such an evader can see the randomness of the universe, but still feels that he is special and just a little beyond the laws of chance. True, he feels other religious experiences reflect expectations conditioned by the culture. Every experience is liable to the dispassionate tools of cold logic and unbiased extrapolation, except his own.

The conceptual avoider's feelings of the validity of experience depends on his dominant mode of thinking. Those who think least about the workings of human thought and who have minimal contact with the nuances of human experience are more likely to take their experience at face value. The businessperson and the physical scientist are just as likely to feel that "God *did* whisper to them in the middle of the night last August" or that a member of their family had been "healed by God." Since they have such little contact with the innumerable similar reports of other people, the experiences still appear to be unique. The egocentric person cannot believe that other people could possibly have the *same* experience, or if they do, it must derive from a different source.

On the other hand, the experienced observer of human thought knows there is an unending stream of profound communions. She is given less insulation. There is no unique characteristic that differentiates her experience from the myriad of others. So the solution is simple: the experience should not be taken literally. Instead, it is a mere symptom of some higher truth of which all human beings have had some measure. The experiences are only indicators of "something" that is there. Mystical interpretations and a persistent search, reinforced on a variable interval schedule by odd and bizarre possibilities, maintain the behavior.

More secular traditions emphasize mind belief. Mind is isolated as a unique "thing," somehow different from the body. The extrapolations usually follow this sequence: "Since mind is different from body, its laws and limits do not apply. Mind may even exist beyond those laws and, by inference, after the body is gone. Since the self and mind are identities, the self may go on in some form forever." Mind believers are God believers, shorn of parental images and removed from religious dogma. They despise behavioristic explanation and regress to solipsism, the oldest and most grandiose tradition of egocentrism.

The powerful contribution of egocentrism to religious experiences and God beliefs is the primary reason they have dominated human behavior. All of us are born with no other reference but ourselves. Without comparisons from other people, we think each private event is unique to us. By the time we reach adulthood, each of us has been exposed to millions of events that have reinforced this belief. Only those events that reward or punish your body directly can be known; the innumerable billions of events, to which the other members of species are exposed, are never noted.

Egocentrism is epidemic in human groups dominated by poverty, religious dogma, and poor education. There is little humanity when people are starving. The basic biological propensities for the survival of the body dominate at the expense of everyone else. With each morsel of food that is eaten, egocentrism is reinforced. The thoughts of personal uniqueness, of special destiny and all other forms of superstitutious thinking that precede the reinforcement are strengthened as well. The struggle for personal survival breeds an uncompromising egocentrism.

Religious dogma encourages egocentrism and feeds on it. Each religion contains the indirect implications that all other religions are somewhat erroneous and that the believer is a little more special. The believer is told that his experiences are real as long as they are interpreted the "right" way. The egocentrism is stroked by phrases, proliferated by every religion (such as "children of God," "true believers," "sons of Allah," "daughters of Christ"). The list seems endless.

Great care is taken by the heads of dogma to prevent exposure to other interpretations. For when this occurs, the convert displays conflict. He realizes that his experiences sound like everyone else's. He comprehends that God Experiences are conspicuous conveniences that occur during personal duress and individual crises. He sees, from the objectivity that occurs only when we watch ourselves in other people, that no matter how much one prays or believes, the laws of nature do not change. Men kill each other unless behavioral principles and understanding are applied. Natural cataclysms are unavoidable, but we can, through the dispassionate analyses and systematic measurements of science, predict when they occur.

These insights require education, and this is lethal to egocentrism. As a person becomes more educated, particularly within the behavioral sciences, he begins to realize that he is not unique. Education forces the egocentric child in each of us to see ourselves as equal to others in human experience. The sacred and profoundly personal experiences that once were proofs of our individual uniqueness are seen for what they are, predictable and necessary behaviors that allow us to deal with the existential terror of personal death and the horror of realizing that we are as vulnerable as everyone else.

Since education is the major antagonist of egocentrism, it is not surprising that the keepers of religious dogma are terrified by the uncensored access to knowledge. There are still attempts to educate with "limitations." In these settings, people are encouraged to take the physical sciences and to learn the logic and methods that predict the world around them. But they are carefully guided away from or are given special procedures on how to predict the world inside of them. The governors who compose the boards of religious colleges and the elders who control the schools for specific sects are cognizant of the organizational devastation that free exposure to the behavioral sciences can unleash.

Certainly education does not always reduce the intensity of the egocentric reference. Those individuals who score high on compartmentalism can maneuver their way through complex challenges of personal significance. This behavioral operation has been discussed in previous chapters. These individuals are characterized by a single factor. What they learn in the classroom stays in the classroom; when they walk out the door, they revert back to the original egocentric organism and religious protagonist. But they are conspicuous and discriminable on examinations when they merely parrot what was said in the textbook or in lecture. However, on examinations that require the *application* of principles to everyday examples of human behavior, they fail, miserably.

Learning about the operations of human experience is a serious procedure that can be as dangerous as experimenting with psychotropic drugs. Very nervous individuals, who score higher than normal on anxiety questionnaires and who ruminate frequently (introversion) can be fragmented by the exposure. These individuals have a history of reducing their anxiety by emphasizing the unique nature of their experiences. When they are exposed day after day or lecture after lecture to the challenge of this assumption, the egocentrism is eroded. The anxiety is elevated.

Anxiety attacks (Harper and Roth 1962; Reiman et al. 1984) arise that are characterized by a feeling of impending doom, a sense of losing one's identity, the fear of losing control, palpitations of the heart, inability to cope with even the simplest of human problems and a sense of hopelessness. It begins with problems with sleeping and failures of concentration. The world appears to be composed of cardboard creatures, and the rich colors that once dominated everyday experiences are replaced by emotionless shades of gray.

The responses to this condition, evoked by the sudden exposure to education, are dichotomous. Escape or avoidance of the situations that produce the experience are most typical. The person drops the course, for example, and defames the content. It was boring or sacrilegious or just plain stupid. In more severe situations, the person may leave the college or university setting totally, and return to some comfortable job that reflects the personality before the challenge.

The rest become quiet mystics with idiosyncratic solutions for their slowly growing existential anxiety. They continue to search in parapsychological lore for some solution. They feel better when reading about escapes through time and space; they are comforted by the anticipation of infinite possibilities that will restore their personal uniqueness. Somewhere, in the future, there will be something, some occurrence, some supreme discovery tht will give meaning to their life and set them aside from all others. They may oscillate between this cosmic dream and a sense of futility, but the old religious ways will never satisfy again.

There are high intercorrelations between neuroticism, anxiety levels, and degree of egocentrism (Tucker 1970). People who are more anxious are usually more neurotic. They are obsessed with questions about whether they are good or bad. They are in constant conflict over sexual urges and aggressive impulses. They may even be apologetic. But above all, they are especially egocentric. Their experiences are real and paramount. The world may face utter obliteration, millions may starve every year; but they ruminate about whether or not they are really bad or really good.

Anxiety (specifically, chronic anxiety) is the second personality characteristic that encourages religiosity. Religious experiences and a stifling system of ritual pervade human cultures whose members are faced with persistent uncertainty. Groups of people living on near-subsistent food sources (such as some of the circumarctic cultures) or amid frequent and devastating earthquakes or tidal waves (such as some of the East Asian and South American cultures), or who are beset by epidemics, are dominated by religious experiences and related ritual. They are means of reducing the extreme existential anxiety induced by the repeated exposures to adverse events.

Reinforcement histories of anxious individuals show similar patterns; they have been exposed to repeated periods of negative stimuli. Their childhoods were an unending but temporally *variable* chain of anticipating punishment and the removal of rewards. They were the ones who had the mothers who threatened punishment days in advance. They were the children who were told that all the good things in their lives would be taken away if they did not display the ideal behaviors that no child could possibly follow. They were the children, who had lost a parent, a dog, or a friend in a seemingly endless chain of adversity.

The God Experience is the pivot around which their normal existence revolves. For if they believe that the God Experience is real and belief in God is correct, then no amount of adversity really matters. Traumas are only tests, examinations, trials, and tribulations that will be exchanged, one for one, for rewards at the end. If the religious experience is real and God is all of space and time, there is no end, no adversity, no unknown. There is no anxiety. The anxiety reduction of the God belief is so rewarding that anything that produces it will be repeated once again.

The neurotic believer can exist only if the religious ritual is simple and the God Experience can never be questioned (Persinger, Carrey, and Seuss 1980).

If the validity of the God Experience as a unique event is challenged, the anxiety begins. With highly anxious individuals whose capability to cope is totally dependent on this belief, the results are predictable and clear. They repress to thinking about it totally; they completely avoid reading about it; they never confront the slightest possibility of doubt. All retorts are graded measures of verbal ritual and stereotyped phrases.

Particular vocations encourage the maintenance of this behavior. However, any job that has a significant portion of unpredictable life-and-death situations over which the person has little control will be pervaded with ritual. The practitioners will be prone to religious experiences and God convictions. Airplane pilots, physicians, and nurses, people on whom rests the responsibility for an inordinate amount of accidental death and adversity, will display more frequent episodes of religious ritual and an above average display of TLTs.

The third major characteristic of the religious person is *suggestibility* (Gordon, 1967). Such trends have been noted within correlational literature. For example, people who are more susceptible to the "sugar pill" or placebo effect are also more religious, more easily hypnotized, and more self-centered or egocentric than those people who are less prone to this effect (Peterson, 1966). They are also prone more to hypochondria, that is, exaggerating or misinterpreting visceral or proprioceptive sensations.

They are frequently sick from a variety of "illnesses" that are never completely cured; instead, they undergo periods of improvement triggered by some new treatment. The significant stages of life are marked by treatments that affect their maladies. Bad backs, stomach problems, headaches, or just feeling bad are common complaints. Not unusually, the strength of the treatment depends heavily on the respect they have for the therapist. The more the therapist is seen within the context of an infallible but friendly source of power (with whom the person has a "special" contact), the more powerful the effect.

The obvious generalization of the parent–child relationship to the therapist, physician, psychologist, minister, or priest strongly suggests the roots of suggestibility. All of us to some degree have been totally dependent at one time on our parents' vocabulary for the labelling of our internal conditions. Parents controlled our private life, when we felt bad or when we were experiencing pain. Most of us were drowned in this verbal flood of suggestion. The theme is evident in phrases such as "You look tired" or "You look sick" or "You must feel happy today."

Of course, the accuracy of their evaluations varied, and this would have influenced the dependence of a person's internal experiences on parental instructions and language. Sometimes the experiences may have been mislabelled. For example, suppose young Jimmy is staring out of the window because he has the first stages of intestinal flu, while young Mortimer is staring out of the window because he has just been infatuated by a pretty girl with pigtails. Both of their mothers, on the basis of the overt behaviors alone, may say, "Gee, you must be in love." Quite obviously, the physiological condition paired with the word "love" would be different for the two boys. In one case, it could be sickening.

If the pairing is done frequently enough and with sufficient systematic occurrence between the same or similar physiological conditions and the same or similar language, then the language can become a conditioned stimulus for evoking those experiences. The child's thoughts and indeed his physiological conditions come under the stimulus control of a source outside of his body: the parent's or parent surrogate's language. Thus, language from another person begins to control the private experiences, the feelings, the anticipations, the expectations, and the sense of wholeness.

The most important implication of this explanation of suggestibility, which will be pursued in the next and final chapter, is the pervasiveness of the control. Our bodies are immense complex loci of behaviors. These behaviors are composed of systems, that is, responses that share a high probability of occurrence. When one response within a response system is displayed, there is a strong likelihood that other responses within that system will be displayed as well. For example, whenever the stress hormones are released, there is also a drop in the person's ability to fight infection because of a general immunosuppression. The two occur together.

The behavioral condition that generates our feelings of awareness or consciousness is only one of those systems. It is correlated with many, but not all of the other systems. There are many examples. Most of us, for example, cannot cause our heartbeat to stop just by thinking about it. Most of us cannot generate massive amounts of antibodies to fight an infection or the flu by simple concentration. The vast majority of us cannot change the distribution of fluids within our joints and alter arthritic pain, or cause other motor pathways to fire and allow listless limbs to function once again. Indeed, there are many systems that are outside of our awareness and our conscious control.

However, these systems may have been at one time within the control of the parents. If physiological conditions were systematically related to the parents' verbal descriptors, then those words, displayed in the appropriate context, could actually *invoke* those experiences. For the adult, the appropriate context would be one that simulated the parent–child relationship. Classic parent substitutes are judges, doctors, lawyers, and other social symbols that control power and place us in a childlike and dependent mode.

Within the emotionally charged context of the church gathering, holy mass, or prayer mat, the suggestible person's experience becomes a function of the language. When the minister frowns on the congregation and lashes them with a sermon full of metaphors, they feel the heat of hell around them. When the preacher begs for them to come forward and give their lives to Christ, the suggestible flooded with the compulsion to run to God and cry at his feet for forgiveness. The less suggestible look on and wonder at the contrived and emotional content of the situation.

Even subtle symbols influence the suggestible person's thoughts and feelings. Chanting with hundreds of others bending on their mats toward Mecca, the believer is struck by the implied equality of all men before Allah. People whose lives have been tormented by repression and social injustice, are converted to the cause. Compelled by the conformity of humans in subjugation, the suggestible person is convinced that all other humans must share the same experience. The poorly studied instincts of human beings gathered in large groups exert their power.

Statistically speaking, there is no one-to-one correlation between our parents' phrases and the exact physiological conditions of our private world. There are necessarily mismatches and contradictions. But there is a continuum (along which we are all distributed) of the relative consistency of the correlation. Suggestibility is highest in those adults who were exposed to a consistent schedule in early childhood and who had been unusually dependent on their parents or some parent surrogate for the control of their behavior.

A consistent and ritualistic schedule would have fostered more or less the same stimulus patterns and similar responses in the environment of the child. This would have allowed the parents' phrases, especially if the repertoire were composed of fixed forms and redundant descriptions, to have been applied to a similar psychological state of the child time and again. The more frequent the pairings between the phrases and the experiences, the more powerful becomes the language for controlling adult experiences within the context of helplessness or childlike subjugation.

For most children, fixed stimulus patterns and ritualistic responses are relegated to specific times or types of behaviors. Plasticity and spontaneity are rarely encouraged or allowed. Those few fixed patterns, starting from early infancy, include religious ritual, responses to parents, and "serious" situations, especially death. Experiences evoked under these conditions and tied to a parent's verbal labels remain sensitive to manipulation. Parental symbols can control those old images and actually cause them to be displayed, often unimpeded, within the adult's private experiences.

From a purely species perspective, suggestibility has clear survival value; it allows a large portion of a population to be maintained by the persistent stimuli of a few. Suggestibility could be argued to arise as an artifact from the shared necessity to have parents who control our early lives and who give us the verbal labels by which we measure our own thoughts and emotions. The conspicuous loading of hypnotic phenomena by verbal phrases and language factors is an expected property. Not only does language label our private behaviors, it also is the most persistent stimulus form by which our parents controlled our behaviors.

Behavioral principles indicate that specific responses are reinforced by their consequences, but this concept also works for general operations. If a particular pattern of stimulus and response presentations (even though they may be quite different in detail) is presented during childhood, then this entire pattern could be rewarded as well. One of the most persistent patterns, which can become discriminative stimuli or cues for the display of hypnotic prodromes, is the dominant parent/submissive child situation. As mentioned earlier, any situation that simulates this old condition in the adult's life can precipitate the suggestible condition.

The suggestible adult displays all of the major features of the religious person. He or she is marked by egocentrism. When a metaphorical stimulus is observed, such as a cool glass of milk slowly pouring from a pitcher, the person may want a glass of milk. However, the explanation for this experience will not be, "I saw a glass of milk on TV and now I am thirsty." Instead, the explanation is, "I want a glass of milk because I am thirsty." The external source is seen as autogenic.

Perceptual patterns induce changes within suggestible people. When they see a child on a CARE commercial, they feel sad; many will cry. As the thin, large-eyed child's face dominates the screen, the suggestible person feels compelled to send in some money to help. Many may hear God whisper to them or experience a divine compulsion that pushes them to the cause. In social situations, they are influenced by subtleties; when a dog vomits, they feel sick as well.

They are conformists as long as the principle is not clear. If they are directly challenged by conditions contradictory to their beliefs, then the egocentric reference quickly buffers. They may appear as suddenly defiant and willing to take all adverse consequences in order not to reject their beliefs. Yet, just a few seconds before, they could have been easily lead, by subtlety and suggestion, to the very same condition.

Education is not a protection against suggestibility. University professors, influential writers, and eminent scientists are as prone to this tendency as the less educated. The critical feature that determines the likelihood is the reinforcement history: (1) the relationship to the parents; (2) the degree to which language controls internal physiological responses; (3) the capacity for compartmentalizing concepts; (4) the strength of the ego, that is, the capacity for minimizing anxiety and maintaining behaviors that indicate confidence.

Spiegel and Spiegel, in their excellent book, *Trance and Treatment* (1978), clearly define the features of the *very* suggestible person. Consistent with prediction, they too have noted that the suggestible person readily accepts logical incongruities, is overtrusting and empathetic, and displays a rigid core of private beliefs, a relative suspension of critical judgment, an ability for intense concentration, and an overall obstinance. Although no empirical comparisons between properties of temporal lobe sensitivity and these personality measures have been completed, both are expected to occur within the same sources of variance.

Specific characteristics of the religious person can be predicted by integrating information from the chapters concerned with the temporal lobe. The ultimate neuro-anatomical bases of the God Experience, its intricate involvement with the sense of self, and its perfusion with time and space concepts arise from the nature of the deep structures of the temporal lobe. Logically, one would expect that people with sensitive temporal lobes that are prone to TLTs will also display other behaviors typical of temporal lobe activity.

The extreme forms of temporal lobe sensitivity, temporal lobe psychosis and temporal lobe epilepsy, include the more discriminable groups of behaviors to which all of us are prone. The primary difference between normal people who attend church every Sunday (or those who do not) and the incarcerated temporal lobe condition is a matter of degree, context, and interpretation. Extremes only emphasize the patterns that are lost in the mundane details of daily existence.

Temporal lobe patients are prone to altered feelings of affect (intense meaningfulness, cosmic highs or deep depression), a sense of personal destiny (they are chosen instruments of God), circumstantiality (interpretation of trivial events as having great personal significance), temporal lobe-relevant perceptions (feelings of floating or hearing voices and general depersonalization), distortions of time and space (out-of-body experiences, déjà vu, precognitive impacts), and of course, religiosity, dominated by mystical and philosophical themes (Bear and Fedio 1977; Geschwind 1983; Hermann and Whitman 1984).

The "normal" (nonpsychotic) religious person shows similar behaviors, except that the delusion is inhibited within an expected framework and the details are channelled within social norms. Although the religious experiences are spontaneous, they are not as frequent, occur in specific situations (e.g., in church or during fixed God-contact hours) and are less absolute. They may range from a sense of pleasant communion with the Creator, without concomitant insight, to a feeling of conviction and a compulsion to proselytize. A bizarre sense of "mission" is less likely.

All other themes remain the same. The person who has had a religious experience that she knows was "real" is more likely to take the experience seriously. She is convinced it is real and will not let it be exposed to humor. Although these people are friendly, there are certain fundamental beliefs that you must allow them to display. They have been associated with intense meaningfulness, usually with a conversion experience precipitated during an adolescent identity crisis or during adult dilemmas.

Alterations in affect (emotional tone) are not limited to populations of patients. The religious person who displays temporal lobe sensitivity that is dominated by input from affective brain nuclei is also prone to emotional highs and lows. During the highs, the euphoria dominates, but with a religious connotation; God is in his heaven and all is right with the world. The person shows signs of being supremely happy, almost manic, and may feel thoughts flowing at a fast rate. Reports of subjects who feel themselves to be "inundated with God's goodness," or "high on God," and who embark on endless work schedules are typical. During these periods, the person talks and acts quickly; in controlled settings, this energy is focused on door-to-door visits and attempts to persuade others. The affective instability is reflected in bouts of crying *with smiles* during which the person praises God. Tears streaming from their eyes, they report supreme euphoria.

The sense of personal destiny, an extension of egocentrism, is evident in statements such as, "I know that God has something special planned for me," or "I have been appointed by God to do this," or "I know I was born to help humanity through this particular time of its development." The exact form of the personal destiny and the degree to which delusions of grandeur confound the process may vary, but the emphasis on personal destiny abounds.

Sometimes these people may not realize what the destiny may be, just that they feel there is a special reason for their existence. They are content to wait, sometimes for a lifetime, for that single event, that discovery, that time in history when their destiny will be fulfilled. In a more crude and concrete form, the sense of the personal may occur as a simple expectation of being "one of God's children" and of the ultimate "return home" at the end of life's journey. The latter dominates less creative thinkers who adhere to more constrictive dogma.

The viscosity of the religious thinker and of the repeated God experimenter is evident in the obsession with particular and simpler forms of argument. Although the person may have a university education and, indeed, have finished the highest degrees available, the religious logic is conspicuous by its lack of latitude and its adherence to the same simple-minded form. It is not unusual for the person (when you can get them to talk about it) to actually change the cadence of their normal speech and begin to display a kind of pedantic overtone.

The sudden emergence of the pedantic deliverance is a frequent and surprising feature of those who have religious experiences that they report they know were real. Quiet, unobstrusive individuals suddenly develop the personal strength and extroversion to teach the "truth." Their speech rarely contains qualifying phrases such as "It may be possible that" or "Here is another option." Invariably, the pedantic presentation is one of absolute certainty, primarily composed of scriptural quotes.

For example, one student who sat quietly in a sociology class during the entire year stood up one day and said, "Harmony definitely exists between science and the Bible, since they are products of the same author. I believe that when we see discrepancies between the two, they are the result of incorrect hypotheses on the part of scientists or misinterpretations of the Bible on the part of theologians. Since the scientific method is designed to discover truth and since the Bible is God's revelation of truth, it follows that problems in reconciling science and the Bible are due to illogical conclusions on the part of the interpreters." The discourse was given with deliberation and great confidence. But when the young lady was finished, she blushed, looked around, and quickly left the room.

No matter how many ways you attempt to show the limits of their logic, religious personalities stick to the basic premises. Although they can apply logic to material free of religious content, these people are immediately stifled when the religious experience is involved. One exemplary incident occurred between faculty during a recent discussion (at a well-known university) of the limits of human experience. The dependence of human experience on the construction of the human brain was a central thesis to which everyone adhered. However, when the nature of the God Experience arose, those who had reported religious experiences simply stated that "this was different." Those who continued to talk about the difference simply reiterated, with explanations like "There are things beyond science," "The religious experience is beyond analytical procedures," or "The world is divided [like Gaul] into three parts: mind, soul, and body." The more political attendees were apprehensive of how religious rejection could hurt the public's confidence in the medical profession.

Such contradiction and narrow-mindedness, typical of religious reference, are strengthened by compartmentalization. It generalizes to other aspects of the person's behavior and is clearly demonstrated. They all agree that women should have an opportunity for education equal to that of men, but their wives must follow the dictates of the scripture (and stay at home to reproduce). A typical compartmentalized argument says, "Animals should not be killed for the benefit of humanity," but "I like to eat well-prepared meat." They say yes to statements like "Science and belief in God are not incompatible" and yes to "God is beyond the capability of science to explain." A blatant example is a recent pontiff's declaration, "There will be no women priests," but that one must oppose "discrimination of women by reason of sex."

Because of the intricate association between the meaning of language and the temporal lobe, it is not surprising that words and phrases are important components of the religious personality. This person is stimulated by vivid metaphorical language that reduces anxiety. Declarations such as, "Yea, though I walk through the valley of the shadow of death, I will fear no evil" evoke tingling sensations and a feeling of meaningfulness. Poetry and prose containing esoteric messages, are attractive. Reading these successive streams of verbal stimuli evoke occasional déjà vu-type sensations. The experiences are similar to what you have felt before, but they are not exactly the same. It is the nature of poetry to express common sense in a form that is familiar enough to be comfortable but different enough not to be mundane.

People who report religious experiences or mystical conversions find solace in reading nonreligious poetry as well. When they are depressed, they "feel better after reading poetry or prose." When alone at night, they enjoy the profundity of poetic soliloquies. The themes change with age, from the "what's it all about" compulsion of adolescence to the preparation for finality of old age.

Like the temporal lobe psychotic (Waxman and Geschwind 1974), many people who have had religious experiences feel compelled to write their ideas down. They may keep extensive diaries. Personal diaries or notes are frequent correlates of developmental periods, when religious or mystical experiences are the central focus of the person's behavior. During more stable conditions, which may be associated with religious ritual (such as church attendance) but also with infrequent religious experiences, a hiatus in textual records is more likely.

If they are maintained, a significant change in theme occurs. The content changes from exhilaration and discussion of the relationship between the self-concept and the God Experience, to more mundane descriptions of everyday events punctuated with fixed verbal rituals, such as verses, or quotes from scriptures. There is a loss of spontaneity. Composition is devoid of the complex syntax or the elaborate variations that were wirtten during the religious experience. Whereas abstract words and polysyllabic sequences dominated the bouts of peak experiences, simple sequences and concrete references typify the quiet periods in between.

Depending on education and verbal skills, hypergraphia may change from frank egocentric records of personal events to more elaborate prose, poetry, or literature (Makarec and Persinger 1985). The religious personality may be prone not only to enjoying but writing proverbial forms of expression, such as the Psalms, only dressed in more contemporary idioms. Although the form is invariably pedantic ("this is the way it is"), the theme may shift to more abstract God references, such as "the great cosmic consciousness" or "universal force." Existential anxiety and poetic expressions of death are symptomatic of masked depression.

Widening affect is a sign of the religious personality. Although the numbers of episodes may be greater during the actual period of the experience, the life of the temporal lobe-sensitive person is sprinkled with these transients. This person will bore you with long lists of "proofs" and examples of God's existence. A check in the mail, a chance meeting of a person who knows someone he knows, the odd behaviors of animals, the movement of a tree when others are quiet, an unusual sunset, a bright display of meteors, an accidental ring of the telephone, a peak experience while walking in quiet woods, a prostrate drunk on a metropolitan sidewalk being helped by a young child, two young lovers intoxicated by their mutual ecstasy, or a sweet fragrance from no obvious source are just a few examples that are used by normal individuals as "proofs" of the validity of their religious experience and the existence of God.

Modifications of memory are also evident within the religious personality. They take two forms: discriminative forgetting (or remembering) and actual distortion of memory traces. This individual is prone to remembering only those events that substantiate beliefs and expectations; negative events are forgotten. He only remembers the many proofs of God's existence. The mysteries of nature, the complexity of life, and the problem of human existence, all of which are quite tractable problems when the emotionalism is removed, are seen as proofs. For them, the religious personality has an excellent, even exceptional memory.

Refutations of the belief and of extrapolations of the experience are repressed. The fact that people who have reported profound religious experiences die on the average at the same age as atheists is not contested. The crash of an airplane containing a load of nuns is forgotten. Random death and meaningless homicides are ignored or dismissed with simple rationalizations (it was the devil or it was merely a test of faith). The frightening fact that there is no difference between life processes with or without religious connotations is avoided.

One can detect these denials in the daily behaviors of the religious believer. As he becomes older, there are increasing numbers of "memories" of proofs his beliefs. Invariably, they rise from episodes during childhood or early adolescence. What appeared then, as a simple and mundane occurrence, is slowly embellished with cosmic and personal significance. The capacity for the religious personality to remember events, often *apparently* in great detail (but in forms that are markedly different from contemporary records), is a convenient means of modifying discrepancies between what is believed and what exists.

The major difference between the religious personality and the mystical personality is simply the form in which the details are expressed. God is replaced with "the great force," "cosmic consciousness," or the "abstract of space and time." Eternity is replaced with the return of Nirvana, where the person blends into a pantheistic panorama of what has ever been and what will ever be. Memories of God Experiences become fragments of previous lives and lead to the conclusion that we have lived before. Reincarnation becomes the religion of the temporal lobe transient.

People prone to mystical orientations still display an unstable affect: peak experiences in the early morning hours, feelings that there must be something more to life, and multiple modifications of death anxiety. There is still the conviction of personal destiny, the obsession with nascence themes ("Where am I going and where did I come from?"). Whereas the religious person pours over accepted textual forms, such as the Bible and the Koran, the mystical believer is attracted to ancient esoteric lore: kabbalas, witchcraft, parapsychology, and metaphysical formulations. Like the religious believer, the mystic bases his proof on egocentric reference and personal experience rather than objective measure. Specification of beliefs in a form that is amenable to refutation is avoided with the intensity of a phobia.

The viscosity of the religious thinker is exhibited in his persistence. Mystical aspirations and the means by which they can be obtained become the substitute for religious ritual. The mystic dwells on concepts. He doesn't read but studies each line, for hours at a time, attempting to extract every hidden meaning. When TLTs occur, some words appear "different," and suddenly they are seen to have great significance or as if they are foreign. It is not unusual even for the simplest of words, such as *the* or *be*, to acquire special significance.

Unlike the religious personality, who is dominated by planned behaviors that guide a lifetime, the mystic personality has a less specific direction. Consequently, he or she must seek out a more immediate, esoteric high. The effect is not self-limiting, and so the mystic quickly satiates. Unlike the rewards promised by religion, for which the believer must learn to wait a lifetime, the goals of the mystic personality can be achieved within a shorter perspective. This quick acquisition is followed by satiation.

The results are predictable. Unlike the religious personality, who follows the dictates of scripture, the life of the mystic becomes a pursuit of a series of different highs. Mystics are the converts to new religions, meditation fads, spiritual regressions, and "new age" movements. Mystic personalities are usually more mature and more educated than those who follow more traditional paths. They are also more egocentric, eccentric, and prone to early nonconformity. Not unusually, their youth behaviors contained experiences of "special selection" or "ultimate destiny."

The religious and mystic personalities are more evident in any vocation that emphasizes or capitalizes on temporal lobe sensitivity and instability. Life styles that hinge on hunches, insights, and clever verbal sequences are prime foci of these behaviors. Not unexpectedly, they are found in greater proportions within the ranks of writers and poets. They are epidemic within the ranks of actors and actresses and other imitators of human behavior. Imitation and suggestibility emerge from the same operation.

Hemispheric dominance cannot be ignored. Its most obvious representation is handedness. Individuals who are "natural" left-handers tend to use more of the right hemisphere than the left hemisphere in certain contexts. Whereas the left hemisphere is associated with verbal capacity and particular details of language, the right hemisphere (in general) is associated with patterns and contexts. Sensations of "wholeness" and of "all being right with the world" are more typical experiential correlates of this half of the brain.

Statistically (controlling for educational level), left-handers are more prone to mystical experiences, temporal lobe themes, and particular esoteric philosophical considerations. They are impressed by language patterns and of finding the "true meaning" or interpretations within verbal sequences. Prose and poetry are good sources for inspiration since their meaning is dependent on the pattern of words and how they generalize to corresponding operations in human behavior. *Metaphorical generalization* could be one name for this procedure. A whale pursuing a ship's crew becomes evil closing in on humanity. A young boy's first bear hunt becomes humanity's perilous journey to find the "true" meaning of life.

Metaphorical generalization accounts for most of intuitive knowledge in science and everyday problem solving. The researcher sees the electron moving around the nucleus of an atom and wonders if the rest of the universe is the same. The housewife sees a small ant running in the same circle and projects her own life's pattern upon it. The psychomotor epileptic has an aura of a young boy pulling a stick from a dog's mouth; one day the epileptic actually sees a little girl jerk an ice cream cone from the hands of another, and he has a seizure.

Metaphorical generalization maintains the pseudosciences that comprise the folklore and myths of twentieth century civilization. They are primarily rewarded because the hidden patterns of two different phenomena involve shared similarities; such convergence reduces the uncertainty and releases the "a-haw" of amygdaloid meaning. In palmistry, the weak personality is seen in the overflexible fingers on the hand. In religious literature, parables and stories contain sufficient permutations that at least one will be close enough to the reader's own behavior. The similarity is seen as wisdom ("there is just something about it that is true").

Left-handers are not the only individuals prone to the properties of the right hemisphere; certainly, to some extent, we all have these potentials. People who emphasize this function are just more obvious in their expression. They are rewarded for pattern more than detail, and perspective more than composition. Musicians, artists, architects, and abstract thinkers of any kind use it well. But the maintenance of these properties within the life style is more important than at the job. The housewife who prefers the organization of the house over its components, the enjoyment in the pattern of the table center rather than the consumption of the meal would also express the properties of the right hemisphere.

Again, I reiterate the caution of talking in terms of a "religious personality"; the concept of personality is a multivariate problem. The same behavior can be evoked by many different stimuli. People may attend church out of habit, for example, because of a mystical experience, due to social pressure, or as a means of simple comradery. Still others may appreciate the music, the prose, or even the company. Religious gatherings are, after all, also collections of human primates; there is the option for social interaction.

In addition, people who report religious or mystic experiences, who attend church, or engage in some similar group behavior are also not necessarily psychotic. These themes can emerge within a God Experience, but they are quite independent processes. Religious experiences are normal and for the most part rational adjustments to the potential incapacitation of existential anxiety. The descriptions and predictions described in this chapter have dealt with normal people who have never had nor will have any significant psychiatric history.

The behaviors noted in this chapter can be discerned within any group of people. But to discriminate them clearly, commitment to religious rituals must be differentiated from a history of religious or mystical experiences. The two types of response profiles may be maintained by different contingencies and be associated with different types of personality patterns. One convenient procedure found by this researcher is to group people on the basis of church attendance (of at least once a week most months) separately from those who attend church less than once per month, and those who report a religious or mystical experience that they know was real, from those who do not.

These criteria result in four groups (Persinger 1984b). Group 1 is composed of people who have never experienced a religious behavior or any significant event (yet) and who do not attend church or some related ritual meeting regularly. The age of this group is loaded toward the young; as the population becomes older and the progression of temporal lobe sensitivity increases, more and more members from this population drift into one of the other three groups.

Group 2 involves people who report religious or mystical experiences that they know were real; however, these people do not attend church regularly. Typically, they are the most eccentric of the four groups. Members emphasize mystical metaphors and use a variety of abstract substitutes for God Experiences, such as time travel, or an unusual psychological "addiction" to science fiction and related forms of fantasy. Invariably, they have dabbled in meditational techniques, parapsychological literature, and esoteric knowledge of some kind.

They demonstrate no obvious signs of neuroses (or psychoses) as defined by both overt behaviors and by answers on questionnaires. For example, they are no more phobic than the normal population. However, they are more egocentric than the first group, as defined by their responses to questions that emphasize social superiority or a relative infallibility of the self over others. They are open to "liberal thinking," such as the possibility of ESP, life on other planets, or that poltergeist or hauntings may involve processes as yet unspecified. There is one compelling theme: "There is an eternal and infinite force."

There are several factors that contribute to the lack of conventional religious beliefs within Group 2. First, the God Experience usually occurred at times when there was no contemporary church attendance. Consequently, the behaviors that immediately preceded the God Experience, such as introspection, meditation, occult practices, or psychedelic pursuits, were reinforced. Interestingly, the latter God Experiences do not occur at the peak of major psychotropic intoxication, but during the "afterdischarges" or "flashes" that are displayed (usually) within the early morning, hours, days, or even weeks later.

These individuals are also prone to multiple God Experiences. Individuals from the other groups have major God Experiences once or twice in a lifetime; they are sufficient, as in the case of Billy Graham, allegedly to determine the person's life forever. These single events are inflection points for maintained changes in behavior. However, when the God Experience or its close similarities are more frequent, the uniqueness is removed.

Since the God experiencer is more egocentric, orthodox interpretation becomes less important. The covert logic proceeds like this: "Since it does not match the nature of my experiences, only the former must be in error. There must be some other explanation." That "explanation" is invariably earmarked by the idiosyncratic features of the God Experiences. Usually these individuals float along the fringes of radical religious factions that foster frequent God Experiences and emphasize excessive emotional commitment. These groups include pentecostal sects, some Baptist groups, and particularly the charismatic movements within the Catholic church.

The problem with Group 2 individuals is coupled to their lack of social compatibility. Although they can interact well with their peers, they have a general aversiveness to conformity and public hierarchies. Conventional beliefs and religious literature are too disassociated from their personal experiences. Instead, they demand immediate and unique access to a special interpretation. The "universal force" and "cosmic consciousness" are the mystic's substitutes for Jehovah or Allah.

Group 3 includes people who attend church regularly but who have never had a mystical experience. These individuals score high on scales of social attractiveness that measure tendencies to display behaviors that look good in public; they are prone to more conformity and social affiliation. They are less flexible in their thinking and rarely considered creative by others. They are usually much more phobic and obsessive-compulsive than the first two groups. Fears of earthquakes, tornadoes, and lightning are more frequent. There is a preference for repetitive tasks, such as sewing, card playing, or watching TV. Jobs that are well defined in scope and expectation are considered more attractive.

For these individuals, religious belief becomes a convenient buffer against life anxiety; the buffer grows with each year of repeated ritual. It runs as a continuous thread through behavioral time, despite the necessary, unexpected adversities of failure, death, and disaster. As friends come and go, interests wax and wane, preferences are acquired and then extinguished, the religious ritual becomes the only remaining constant; it *is* the personality. A religious experience, if it occurs (usually later in life and only if the ritual does not relieve the anxiety) merely imbues the belief with special meaning and cosmic proof of its validity.

The fourth group involves people who attend church regularly and who report religious experiences that they know were real. These individuals tend to score higher on questions that would classically reflect personality disorders on popular clinical inventories. For example, these individuals are more likely to report, often with great pride, that Christ has appeared to them in a vision or that God has healed a member of their family, or that they are a special agent of God.

These individuals usually have had one or two God Experiences that have been interpreted within the framework of belief. Unlike Group 2, there is a minimal discrepancy between the belief structure and the details of the God Experience. Regular churchgoers who have had a religious experience, especially those over 40 years of age, have learned to label their varying experiences. The early morning highs are "God's presence," the adversities of life are merely "tests of faith," and the occasional paranormal events are "gifts."

Even the types of details are compatible with the *expected* forms of social behavior. God may talk to you; this is normal. But you do not talk to God. You may pray to him or show some childlike subjugation, but you cannot be his equal. There is no evidence of any classical psychotic process. In the latter case, there would be a confusion of roles and a bizarre component to the details. God and the person would be equals (or the same). A trivial event such as a newscaster saying, "Today the world was wrought with turmoil" would exact an aura of "holy inspiration." People in Group 4 still say no to statements such as "I am God," "A force leaves my body that makes people do what I want them to do," or "I am possessed by evil spirits."

There are also first-order differences between churchgoers, regardless of having had a religious experience or not, and those who do not attend church. No significant differences are evident between Catholics and Protestants, except that there is a tendency for Catholics to attend a social service more frequently. Churchgoers as a group are more likely to be right-wing and totalitarian in the application of their dogma. Southern Baptist ministers, for example, score precariously high on fascist scales.

People who attend church regularly are more likely to agree (by both their vocal and public behaviors) with classic dogma statements, such as, "Everything is turning out the way the prophets said," and "The second coming of Christ is near." They are also more prone to some frightening applications. Statements such as, "If God told me to kill I would in his name," and "People should be guided for their own spiritual good," are considered compatible with religious expectations.

Regular church attenders are more deliberate, cautious, worrying, and guarded than nonattenders. Although they are mannerly, they are methodical and rigid. Typically, they are quite formal in their mode of analyses and show pedantic thinking. They are invariably overly deferential to authority, custom, or tradition. If they have had a religious experience, they are likely to be more easygoing, but they are still defensive. They frequently may be seen as shallow or unambitious. The latter type is antagonized by a childhood of low socioeconomic status combined with a family environment that encourages nonachievement. Their lives are characterized by a lack of self-direction (outside of religious references) and a lack of self-discipline.

People who report religious experiences, regardless of church attendance, also share behaviors relative to those people who do not report a religious or mystical experience and either attend or do not attend church regularly. The experiencers are more prone to keeping diaries and feeling refreshed or comforted after reading or writing poetry or prose. They are more likely to report belief in a ubiquitous God matrix and to agree with statements such as, "Two or three times in my life, there have been brief moments when I felt very close to a Universal Consciousness," or "At least once in my life, I have felt the presence of another Being."

The experiencer population can be further subdivided, regardless of church attendance, with regard to an ontogenetic factor: those individuals who had their first religious or mystical experiences before they were teenagers, versus those whose first conviction came later. Those who report (and remember) earlier religious or mystical experiences are likely to score higher on the psychotic scales and the measures indicative of temporal lobe sensitivity or instability.

Interestingly, early onset of temporal lobe epilepsy is more likely to herald later psychotic processes.

People who report an early experience are more prone to confusion between the sense of self and the God Concept. They agree with statements like, "I am a special agent of God" or have a perverted interest (if they are not churchgoers) in extraterrestrial forms. These individuals are more likely to report that they are "star children" or "a spirit" from a super race (who watches over humanity). They have a special mission that is yet to be revealed. When Jehovah or Allah is replaced by their space-age surrogates, sons and daughters of God are no longer in fashion. Instead, they may become the "spiritual inseminations of superior intelligence from distant galaxies." Except for the delusion, they are as normal as any other God believer.

More traditional delusions involve reincarnation and the conviction of having lived or of still living other lives. People who have had their first mystical experience before they were teenagers are more likely to agree with statements such as "Although I am not totally sure, there is a good possibility that I have lived a previous life." This type of thinking is more likely among people who maintain jobs that demand radically different patterns of behavior that must be compartmentalized to maintain the person's stability. Theatre is one obvious refuge.

People who report early religious experiences but who continue attending church demonstrate the same degree of peculiarity, except that the form is modified within accepted dogma. These individuals, when they talk candidly, admit that they sometimes feel they may be the sons of God. Frequently, they report consequent visitations from angels or spiritual creatures. Whereas the non-churchgoer in this category is more likely to agree with the statement, "As a child, I played with an imaginary playmate," churchgoers are more likely to recall that "a guardian angel or Mary" appeared from time to time to reiterate their importance.

The religious or mystical experiencer, regardless of church attendance, also scores high on a variety of statements that reflect a general parapsychological cluster (Persinger, 1984c; Persinger and Valliant, 1985): "Once I thought about a person whom I hadn't seen for a while and then saw the person a few minutes later"; "Sometimes I can read another person's thoughts"; "I have experienced things that were about to happen before they happened"; "I have seen an apparition of a recently deceased loved one."

Although people who have had their first religious experiences before they were teenagers are more likely to report parapsychological references, all religious experiencers score higher on this cluster than reference groups. Interestingly, weekly churchgoers, who may insist that people should be guided for their own spiritual development, do not report these kinds of experiences. Instead, they are more likely to cluster them within "an evil format," a response also displayed for anything unusual. The latter is seen in the positive response to statements such as "Poltergeists and haunts are works of the Devil."

However, by far, the most unusual aspect of the religious and particularly the mystical experiencer is the generalized and increased frequency of temporal lobe signs. Individuals who report they have had religious experiences that they know were real also experience a variety of feelings, sensations, and compulsions that reflect temporal lobe sensitivity. Both experiencers and non-experiencers are more likely to report statements such as "I have dreams of floating or flying through the air at least once a year" or "When relaxed or just before falling asleep, I sometimes feel pleasant vibrations moving through my whole body."

Religious or mystical experiencers are more likely to report other statements that are not included in the usual repertoire. ("At least once in my life, very late at night, I have felt the presence of another Being"; "Sometimes in the early morning hours between midnight and 4:00 a.m., my experiences are very meaningful"; "After my religious conversion, I suddenly felt full of energy"; "When I walk upstairs, I sometimes note a strange smell from nowhere.").

The religious personality can be (and usually is) a normal person by all accepted definitions. Like the population from which much of these analyses were derived, the prone personality has friends and children at home. He may be a hard worker and a dedicated father. She may be a responsible mother and a fundamentally good person who loves humanity. He or she may have great intellect, capable of powerful but specific analyses. Their apparent stability may dominate, usually in a conspicuous manner.

A religious personality is neither good nor bad in itself. It is no more good or bad than an extrovert, an introvert, a sensitizer, or a repressor. It is a consequence of reinforcement history and the conditions that contribute to temporal lobe sensitivity. Together they are solutions to daily apprehensions that slowly accumulate over a lifetime (existential anxiety).

The religious or mystical personality is characterized by a syndrome, that is, a collection of behavior patterns. They include compartmentalization, suggestibility, egocentrism, viscosity, dependency on the literal interpretation of words and the experience of temporal lobe sensations. Some of these patterns may be more evident in some individuals than others; the critical criteria are: (1) the number of these behaviors that are displayed and (2) the frequency of their occurrence. The details, which range from being God's children to observing the reincarnation of an ant, are a matter of cultural detail.

These patterns are optimal in specific contexts. Viscosity of thought and behavioral perserveration facilitate the discovery of fine details. The greater the technical nature of a science and the more intricate the workings of the phenomena, the more effective the viscous thinker can become. Her perseveration despite its redundancy, ultimately finds a solution. Many physical sciences have become prone to this feature; it is not surprising that some of the most irrational God believers have emerged from these fields. But within the appropriate context, the propensity has a function.

The ability to string together pleasant words or to coin clever phrases during oceanic experiences and peak inspirations can sway the moods of millions. Literal interpretation of what other people say and the quiet presumption of their validity can create endless associations. But the builders of semantic castles in the air quickly flounder in the mass of complex detail. They panic when confronted with phenomena to which there are many contributions. Statistical analyses become unfathomable and hence untrustworthy. Multivariate causes turn the world of black and white into endless shades of gray.

When does the religious personality become dangerous to himself? Impulsivity is optimal for survival in a hostile environment, but it is catastrophic amid the cold, contrived inhibition of the business world. A sensitizer can find great insight when the world is comfortable around him; in the midst of continuous anxiety, he freezes into mediocrity and fear. The sender of nonverbal cues makes a great surgeon but a poor social worker. The receiver has great empathy but is sick at the sight of blood. When does the religious personality become dangerous to society?

10
The Good, the Bad, and the Uncertain

If the God Experience is an artifact of transient changes in the temporal lobe, and religious behaviors are maintained by the classic principles of conditioning, are the consequences really that serious? The rabid believer would not be concerned with these demonstrations, since he or she would be safe within the reflex arc of "God created everything, so of course, He can be experienced through the brain; of course, the laws of animal behavior, in general, apply to human beings as well." The implications that God Experiences and religious rituals are evolutionary consequences of neural organization are smothered in some teleological context.

But the problem cannot be dismissed that easily. If God Experiences are what they appear to be (inspirations from the Creator), then their neuronal basis is little more than another demonstration. If *God Experiences are creations of temporal lobe transients* colored by conditioned images, then there is much greater concern. The process that precipitates the God Experience may also contain some fundamental flaw that could eradicate us from the face of this earth. This potential may have been in our genetic pool for millenia, waiting to be released by a special sequence of events. They would be the sign stimulus to an innate releasing mechanism.

It would not be the first time that a behavior on which a species capitalized to survive was also the basis for its destruction. The dinosaurs dominated by their massive size; the rapid change in ambient temperature selectively terminated them. They buried their unborn offspring in the sand. From the sun's warmth, the young life forms obtained the energy required for growth. Then the small predators emerged, less dependent on passive heat, requiring fresh flesh to maintain their biochemistry. Dinosaurs became extinct. The genetic propensities that had once sustained their superiority now contributed to their elimination.

The God Experience has had survival value. It has allowed the human species to live through famine, pestilence, and untold horrors. When temporal lobe transients occurred, men and women who might have sunk into a schizophrenic stupor continued to build, plan, and hope. The terror of being "the lonely reed in the universe" (Blaise Pascal) was replaced with the peace of knowing that we are not alone. The anarchy of rampant homicide and indiscriminate slaughter have been checked, at least from time to time, by the anticipation of rewards and the apprehension of eternal punishment.

The God Experience has had survival value. It has allowed people to feel "righteous" as they bashed the skulls of others who dressed a little differently or described God with a foreign accent. When temporal lobe transients occurred, each soldier has felt that somehow he would survive the battle. If they had not occurred, wars would never have been fought. They would have been crushed by the objective confrontation of death as the final end to all of existence. Now people do not have to engage in battle. They can push buttons and dictate instructions to intelligent machines. A quiet conviction can trigger unimaginable cataclysm.

Neither the God Experience nor religious behaviors are either totally good or bad. The value judgment is a matter of perspective. For those who feel that God exists and eternity waits forever, the destruction of other countries at the risk of reciprocal annihilation may be seen as a perverted form of some absolute good. ("Better dead than Red" is one political example.) To those who see the God Experience for what it is, a transient coherence within unstable neuronal strata, the same conviction is viewed as bad. There is no absolute good or God; both are creations of the human brain. It was not created any more than rocks are made from minerals. The brain was not created; it simply occurs and one of its properties is the God Experience.

In this chapter, *good* is defined in terms of what is beneficial for *humanity as a species*; it contains the assumptions that versatility and creativity are more preferred than regimentation and order. It assumes that there is neither right nor wrong, but human beings. Good presumes that the productive lives of people benefit the species more than companies or nations. Good means parents know enough about behavioral principles not to raise their offspring in the same neurotic mold. Good emphasizes survival of *homo sapiens*, not countries or religions or gods. Bad is defined as any contradiction to these conditions.

We begin with the bad. It can be described in a nightmare that haunts any educated and suspecting person. The scenario begins with a few men who control the destiny of humanity. Each one has been conditioned to respond to the jargon of his political system, but each one knows the nature of the game. Among the radicals of the groups who would rather kill everything than be subjugated by the other, there are those who know that their methods do not differ. For the men and women who compose each society, political prejudice by a small totalitarian group or legal manipulation by a few holders of massive wealth are not discernible.

Then the ultimate "answer" becomes apparent, as usual, when it is least expected. Each group is poised, ready for the other's move. Both realize with horror that the result of their decision could be death for the entire planet. But one of them, the more egocentric of the two leaders, feels that God exists and that there is an afterlife. He feels that to save humanity from a perceived evil, all humanity must die. It is not a strong conviction but a hunch whispered in a sudden sense of "knowing." And so with the confidence of inspired knowledge, he pushes the button. The nightmare is finished.

In any complex system, the final response that displaces the moment of the dynamics is miniscule in proportion to the whole. The more complex a system, the smaller the response required to set the motion toward the extreme. Of course, there are the normal feedbacks that usually warn, with each level of increasing instability, that catastrophe is imminent. As defense systems or human organizations become larger and more elaborate, the change moves out of human perspective. There are just too many "things" to see the drift begin; there is just not enough time to allow the decision to be properly evaluated.

Ultimately, the final response is displayed by a human being. It makes no difference who he or she is, a private or president or prime minister. They are still human beings. What will go through their minds when such a decision has to be made? What subtle sequence of assumptions will decide, probabilistically, which way the responses will follow? For a split second, will the hidden belief that God exists and that there is a real hereafter afford the discrete amount of insurance to press the catastrophe?

Religious dogmatists are not the problem; they usually show their preferences and can be easily discriminated. The dangerous person is the recondite religious believer whose God Experience waits for the time of the catastrophe or whose convictions of an afterlife have never been confronted. He is the one who has emphasized a life of social presence and has conformed to what was socially appropriate or expected by his peers. This person has never experienced the consequence of his conditioning and has never labelled it appropriately. When it occurs, for the first time, it will appear real, charged with the sense of the personal and of absolute reality.

History has been replete with episodes of missing the obvious. The human thinker has had a problem seeing things that are closest to himself. First, we quantified the heavens and astronomy emerged; then we measured the earth and geology was born. Next we classified the animals and zoology became systematic. Only in the latest brief era have we dared to measure ourselves. When one is immersed in the very phenomena that are being studied, the needed reference for detecting them is difficult to find. The most full-blown phenomenon could exist right beside you and you would not know.

Social groups, political parties, and military organizations alike screen for personality factors. Sometimes they encourage certain types of individuals. Aggressive, repressive (as opposed to sensitive), compartmentalized, and externally controlled (one's fate is controlled by factors beyond one's control, as opposed to free will) personalities may be preferred for soldiers. They have performed in the past. Introverted sensitizers who have learned to express their impulses in words rather than in violence are predisposed to finding a solution. They seek the answers to the subtle forces that change history.

The role of religious connotations and recondite God beliefs within the objective context of military decisions and political confrontations has not been seriously considered. Despite all of the measures of personality profiles, stress endurance, suggestibility, and social conformity, the hidden danger has only been suspected. It is just this potential within every politician, general, or soldier that will determine the final decision.

The potential results from a pattern of implicit semantic expectations. They are conditioned by *implicit chains* that can be contaminated by the consequences of God Experiences and the presumptions of religious dogma. Although implicit chains have been discussed briefly before, their operation is quite simple. They do not require consciousness or awareness. In fact, that's the danger. The consequences *just occur* as impulses in the person's stream of behavior.

Operationally, an implicit chain is conditioned in temporal sequences. If, for example, a nonsense word like word RUMP is paired with the word ESP, then the occurrence of the RUMP will evoke the expectation of ESP. Some number of trials are required to reach a criterion of accuracy for a dozen of similar pairs. If later the word ESP is paired with SUK, then the presentation of ESP elicits the expectation of the letters SUK. A number of trials are also required to reach criterion.

Now, one pairs the word RUMP and SUK. After a few pairings, not surprisingly, the presentation of the nonsense letters SUK evokes the expectations of RUMP. But there is a difference. Significantly fewer trials are required to accurately make the association, even though the two words have never been paired together before. The connections between the other words, the intermediate stages, have facilitated the learning. Those connections are the implicit chains.

The implicit chains pervade the gut feeling of bad and good. Their operations never end. The roots begin during earliest childhood and their links extend for the length of one's life. They influence our feeling about other people and our responses to words or ideas. They dominate our first impressions and infiltrate our hunches, intuitions, and insights. An example emphasizes this point.

Young Jenny begins her life like every other little girl. The experience of pain: an intense slap on the wrist or spanking is paired with the word "bad." The pairing is quick and repetitive as the mother holds her little hand and strikes it, each time saying "bad." It is fused with the negative affect of pain and the compulsion to avoid its contact ever again.

Years later, young Jenny hears the word "sex." Her parents talk about it late at night when they think she is asleep. When she asks, "What is sex?" the mother becomes very solemn and avoids it, thus displaying the behaviors associated with punishment or aversion. In more blatant instances, the mother may simply say that "Sex is bad" or "Sex is evil." Love may be fulfillment, but sex is bad. Thus, the pairing occurs between "sex" and "bad."

Jenny grows into an adolescent and becomes interested in boys. So Jenny asks her mother about her feelings. The mother explains the difference between men and boys. "Men," the mother says, "are only interested in sex." They don't care about you, your true self. They are only interested in sex." Thus the word "man" becomes paired with sex and its connotations.

Jenny graduates from high school and attends a large university. The students are rich, new sources of stimulation. One day, while eating lunch by herself in the cafeteria, a pleasant face pokes its way into her vision. She is startled; she focuses and perceives the most handsome person she has ever seen. He sits down in front of her and they exchange the feelings of adolescent infatuation.

The relationship grows and Thanksgiving approaches. Jenny asks her boyfriend home to see the parents. Excitedly, she introduces Jason to her parents. The Thanksgiving dinner goes smoothly and they spend the hour exchanging glances across the table. With the dinner ended, Jason is asked to join the father in the living room for a quiet cigar and some "men's talk." Jenny and her mother stay behind to clean the table and wash the dishes.

Jenny waits for a few minutes to hide her excitement. Then she asks her mother, "Well, what do you think of Jason?" The mother smiles and looks over at Jenny and replies, "Jason is a very nice person, but he is a man." Nothing else is said, but slowly Jenny drifts into an uneasy feeling. Jason's shining armor becomes tarnished.

Now when Jenny looks at Jason, she sees the dark stubble on his face. His innocent touch of her body is now reconnaissance to check for further possibilities. His mooning look becomes a ploy to rob her most cherished possession. The consequences of the implicit chains, slowly shaped over decades and maintained by multiple associations, change the good into the bad. Awareness is not essential. Intelligence is not always a guard against it. Implicit chains work at the preverbal level. Since they exist in increments of time, much larger than the periods that compose our sense of the present, we cannot easily see them. We are lost in the trees and cannot see the outline of the forest.

Implicit chains can condition gut responses through inference and by generalization. They lie at the core of prejudice and emotional repugnance. Implicit chains create the conflict between what we should and do feel. One classic example involves the basic association between evil and darkness, between bad and black. There are many other factors that control prejudice; this is one example of how implicit chains contribute.

The association begins, innocently enough, because of the nature of the world around us. When we are young, we are punished for dirt on our clothes. Many times there is a pairing between the word "bad" and the dark dirt on light skin. Within the obsession of cleanliness, where a shining white sink and toilet are signs of good and comfort and where a clean, sparkling floor is some people's final aspiration, anything black (and hence dirty), creates a sense of repulsion. Black is bad and light becomes good.

It's an old observation that goes back into human history: black is bad; darkness is evil. Darkness inspires anxieties about things that cannot be seen; the night is full of strange perceptions and altered states; it is the natural projection test for the horrors of imagination. Light is good. Things can be seen in the light, there is nothing hidden. It smells bright and fresh. It is a time of activity and sunshine, of warmth and enjoyment; the dark, the black, is a time of coldness and death where one imagines how the grave might be.

The most common implicit chain moves in this direction. Pain is paired with the word "bad." The word "bad" is paired with situations that contain dirt or blackness. Blackness is compared by definition or through observation with the word "negro." The implicit chains lead to further associations. Somehow, the black person appears dirty; he or she may even appear bad. Even some people who have had minimal contact with melinated skin (which is really not "black" in a technical sense), report negative gut responses. Sometimes the chains can be neutralized, but the process is complicated. Equal amounts of positives do not cancel negatives. "Black is beautiful" can change the implicit chains into a positive direction, but the aversive connotations of "black" and "dirty" rest on a wide base of incidental learning.

Chains are so fundamental to our mode of thinking that they dominate our logical structure. The formal statement, "All men are mortal; Mike is a man, therefore, Mike is mortal," is a chain. First, "mortal" is paired with "man." Second, "Mike" is paired with "man." Even though there is no direct connection in either semantic space (within the same sentence) or perhaps even in time (the two sentences could be learned in separate episodes), the imminent and unescapable conclusion remains that Mike is mortal. Inclusion of the word "all" is a semantic substitution for the entire set of possibilities; it is another form of everything.

Religious belief begets helplessness during crises. It is not intentional, necessarily, but a conditioned consequence of implicit chains. One cultural theme has been: "God, an omnipotent and omniscient force, exists"; "God looks over humanity and protects each person"; "When all else fails, pray to God and He will give the answer." These are ideas that most of us have heard and many of us believe.

Now suppose a conflict has begun. There are still options for preventing a catastrophe, but the mechanism is too complex; the solutions are not obvious. There are just too many variables involved, and a sense of helplessness creeps into the situation. Implicit chains constrain people from pursuing the problem. As opportunities pass by forever, the person waits for some sign of deliverance. All else has failed and now expectations, conditioned by the nuances of a life of language learning, become the decisive variable. The system drifts, escalating as it changes, toward the final extreme.

The greatest evil is the most dangerous. God Experiences and religious passivity are more likely to occur during crises. There is a lethal difference between practicing for national conflict or imagining the end of humanity and the actual events that start the final countdown. It's like knowing that your grandfather or grandmother is going to die and rationalizing what it means. But when he or she finally dies, even if you are miles away and do not see the body, the images of the person dominate your twilight states. Even if you are not a sensitizer but a person who suppresses the imminence of death, the images of the person who just died creep into your free associations. It's the nature of verbal conditioning and the way we learn to handle death.

During the actual crisis or conflict, when conditions make nuclear war imminent, God Experiences could shift a decision. We do not know how many of those individuals who control our final destiny will suddenly feel "what should be done." How many will be incapacitated by the sounds of God "telling them what to do"? How many of them will be incapacitated by the TLT as the number of options for avoiding a predictable end approaches zero? How many will push the button or give the command along the fatal chain of all-or-none conditions, with the sense of personal conviction that God has inspired this final test of humanity's worth?

These questions are not academic exercises or sensationalism. They are as real and as profound as any existential issue that humanity has yet confronted. We, as a species, have the capacity to totally alter the future of the planet, either in a single series or in endless episodes of gradual destruction. The third planet from an average star could become as lifeless as all the others.

The contemporary condition is *not* comparable to any previous time. During previous conflicts, when death seemed imminent, there was always the hope of survival in some form. Although you may die, your sons and daughters could continue on in some distant place. There was always the chance of life. The enemy, also a human being, may capture you and you could avoid the holocaust. Even in the most desperate situations, there was also the small possibility that somehow, after the battle, you would still be moving among the carnage. But now, such options are gone.

Can we attenuate the risk of subtle thoughts and God Experiences contributing to the demise of our species? The answer is a definite *yes*! We can curb the influence of this potential. By studying religious behavior in *objective contexts*, we can isolate and identify the conditions that precipitate it. By allowing God Experiences to be analyzed, removed from the protection of sacred presumptions, we can understand how the mechanism works. Of course, there is a matter of privacy involved, but if a man in a crowd holds a bomb in his personal possession, do we ignore it for the sake of his "privacy"?

The objective evaluation of religious behaviors will be difficult and will be met with great resistance. It will challenge the sense of special selection and impugn the egocentric reference. Since political ideology feeds from the same source as religious affiliation, that power will be threatened as well. Within the dispassionate and analytical light of scientific investigation, the insulation between the contingencies of political manipulation and the operations of religious conviction will be removed. Ethnocentricism, the feeling that our country or culture is just a little better than all others, will be seen as a symptom of this syndrome.

To survive, we must eliminate the convenient reliance on egocentric reference as the proof of experience. We must see ourselves, each one of us, for what we are: biochemical systems that display behavioral patterns. We are all subject to the laws of conditioning. Our individual experiences are no more unique or special than the grains of sand on a beach. It's a matter of perspective. There is certainly a small measure of peculiarity, overexaggerated to elaborate our identities, but the crucial behaviors do not differ. In the large scale of observation where humanity exists in zoological time, the individual doesn't matter.

To continue, each man and woman must know that everyone else also feels their God Experiences are just as real and valid. We must realize that they are products of our brain's construction. We must understand that certain questions such as "Who created humanity?" may be as nonsensical as "Do you walk to work or take your lunch?" Each of us must learn to recognize that when gods appear in times of personal duress, the brain has displayed another one of its properties. Like the healing process of a superficial wound, the God Experience allows the survival of the system from which it has arisen—the sense of self.

To remain, we must face and refute the impulse to accept the varied forms of religious persuasion. It would be nice to believe that there is Someone there that knows *your* name and who listens to *your* needs, and who is interested in *your* problems. But despite the good intentions of the people who propagate the myth, it must be seen for what it is. Like the sense of free will, it is a property of the human brain. The sense of self will *not* survive the heat of the thermonuclear blast any more than ideal circles spin in Platonic space.

The counterargument has been and will be some form of the empty theory of faith. You may be told that faith is required and cannot be substantiated by scientific means; you simply must believe. Faith is just another word for stroking the egocentric sense. It heaps the onus on the believer and dares him to indict himself. Most people have not had the courage to face it.

In more desperate times, faith is reified. People have actually believed that faith is some measurable quantity that can exert influence on the activities of nature (Browning 1968). Faith cannot move mountains; it never could and never will. Faith only maintains the behaviors that can. But if the behaviors are demeaned and their interpretations are distorted by egocentric fantasies, the brink will be brought much closer.

It will be the egocentric man who will kill us in the end. He will be the American who is gullible enough to believe the propaganda that the Russian is a barbarian who somehow is not human. He will be the Russian who believes the Kremlin rhetoric that Americans are deviates who have vowed to destroy them because they will not be subjugated to political illusion. He will be the Third World Man whose brain, ravaged by a history of malnutrition and chronic disease, creates the revelation of how God's, Allah's, or the Great Kahuna's will should be done.

The dangerous properties of the God Experience and religious thought can be defused by more precise understanding of the implicit chains that guide their occurrence. The semantic time bomb that has ticked away in our species, from the first utterance of symbols as substitutions for the reflex world of events, can be understood by the precise study of the kind of person that believes in religious anticipations. Like the hurricane, we will not be able to stop it. But, but knowing how it works, perhaps we can prevent the people who may cause it from getting into the situations where they can.

There are good components of the God Experience that may be used for the benefit of humanity. The first is rooted in the fundamental fact that every person must have a parent or parent surrogate during a major proportion of development. From these surrogates, labels are obtained for private experiences. In addition to labeling our overt behavior, such as we are acting "bad," "like an ass," "good," or "proper," we learn to pair words with our feelings and internal states. These words and their associated processes become our "thoughts" and the major components of our stream of consciousness.

The positive component is due to the existence of response systems. Each person can be considered a locus of behaviors, a three-dimensional space within which behaviors have a very high probability of occurrence. A response is any change in space that can be pointed to, counted, and checked by inter-observer agreement. A response system is defined in terms of the shared probabilities of the responses that compose it. The occurrence of one response in a system is associated (sooner or later) with the display of the other responses within it. The critical feature of a response system is not similarities in how responses look, but when they *occur* in time.

There are several types of response systems. Many of them are associated with traditional labels of the body's organization. They compose the disciplines of the life sciences. For example, the heart system is associated with changes in the vascular tissues. When the heart rate increases, there is also a change in the size of the capillaries, in the diameter of arteries, and in the speed of blood through its containers. The occurrence of one of these responses is very likely to be associated with the display of others.

One response system can come under the control of another through conditioning. The learning operation is quite simple and is based on temporal contiguity. If the reward or reinforcement associated with the occurrence of one response system is dependent on the occurrence of another, then there is a tendency for the first to occur only when the other is present. There may not be any actual causality involved, that is, the presence of the second system may not actually be required for the reinforcement of the first to occur (although such an operation would certainly strengthen any effect). The critical feature is temporal contiguity.

Most of us cannot influence our heart rate by simply thinking about it. The primary reason is that the reinforcement, the drop in heart rate, has not been paired with "thinking" about it in a systematic manner. If every time you thought to yourself "slow heart rate" you saw the heart rate actually slow down (were reinforced), then the thoughts would become a conditioned or discriminative stimulus for the heart rate change. You could say that the heart rate has come under the control of a cluster of thinking responses. In the context of our definition of response system, the heart rate has also become a component of "awareness behaviors."

"Awareness" and "consciousness" are words that are applied to a special kind of response system that is composed primarily of covert responses or thoughts. They cannot be seen directly, but can be inferred by the movements in the larynx and electrical changes in the ideomotor regions of the cerebral cortex. When you ask people to read prose and poetry silently for several hours, a common report is a sore throat or stiff larynx muscles, even though they did not say anything. There is a close relationship between the muscles of speech and the experience of reading words.

However, thoughts are components of only one of many response systems within the body. Although thoughts can control some systems due to genetic or learned factors, all response systems are not affected equally. You may be able to move your hand in response to the imperative sentence, "Move your hand," but you cannot cause your ACTH levels to decrease if you are under stress when the instruction "Make yourself relaxed" is given. You cannot reverse the course of time and regenerate the physiology of youth through will.

There are many response systems within the body volume that are outside the influence of "consciousness" or "awareness" (von Eckartsberg 1981). In fact, by necessity, there must be some that operate *only* when consciousness is not displayed. There must be those systems, reciprocals of awareness, that occur when the sense of self-awareness sinks beneath deep delta sleep. When the awareness terminates each night, the trillion cells of the body still continue. Their correlates, whatever they may be, are maintained across the amnesic blackness of sleep.

There has been one condition that has had the potency and the pervasiveness to control every system within the body. This can be called the *parental operation*. Every system within the body ultimately was dependent on the parent or parental surrogate for maintenance. The effect may have been accidental or contrived. But the early locus of behaviors that you later learned to call "myself" has been under the control of parents. They became generalized reinforcers because they were the constant stimuli accompanying the words that we used to label our thoughts and feelings.

No matter how much you try, there are systems that are beyond self-manipulation. Since these systems, such as the control of water balance, have never been displayed at the same time as consciousness (that is, you have never been aware of them), they function independently of your control. However, at one time, they were under the stimulus control of parental patterns. Parental patterns were the sources of milk; they were the concomitants of fluid loss.

For the adult, these patterns are manifested in a social context, in situations where the person is compelled but never persuaded to exist within a dependent framework. Adult equivalents of parents are lawyers, judges, psychologists, physicians, and police officers. They may also be religious leaders, political persons, or individuals who display great social insulation and much inferred power.

As long as the person never knows them personally, the magic is maintained, as it is between the parent and the child. If the person recognizes or realizes the two as equals, that the parental image is also limited and unsure, the phenomenon will not occur. As long as the person expects that there is some greater power that guides the decision of the politician, physician, or psychologist, the response systems that were once under the control of the parent will remain manipulable by the surrogate.

It is essential to satisfy the expectation of roles. There is a trivial example that clearly demonstrates the importance and power of appearances. One young graduate student decided to "be a peer of her patients." She greeted them in the office with faded jeans and talked in casual conversation. The turnover in her clients was alarming. They would visit her once and then remark that they felt she could not help them at all. Her self-esteem suffered as well. She changed her mode of presentation. She began to wear dresses and makeup. She greeted her patients warmly, but in a professional manner. She talked in technical language that appeared quite clear, but which was punctuated from time to time with hidden connotations. The patients returned and the caseload became stable. They commented, often in written recommendations, that she is one of the best clinicians they had ever experienced. She was essential to their well-being.

The power of parental patterns is prevalent around us. Think of the people whose sense of self is almost a total function of their peers. When they ignore him, the person is miserable. When they include her, the person feels complete. When they reject him, the person contemplates suicide. He hates himself for no apparent reason; she despises herself without a casue. The parental patterns, generalized to the comments of the group, control some people's sense of self. How much physiology and biochemistry is controlled as well? Does the rejection translate into ulcers? Does the derision generate muscle tension deep within the shoulders? The covert systems of the body are not quiet. Beneath the surface, there is an endless storm of physiological perturbations.

The power is evident in the dozens of therapies and religions that rise and fall with each generation. In addition to their novelty, there is one other major ingredient: the parental person. His or her characteristics are predictable, depending on the age of the group. Leaders are invariably old enough to be the parents of the people who follow. The parental person is seen as wise and infallible. His actions are beyond the control of ordinary people and sanctioned by some higher authority. He controls the rewards and punishments for the sense of self.

There have been cases where people walked when told by priests, when lymphomas shrank when the physician gave the trusting person only sugar water. There have been instances where myelin re-eroded when the minister was found to be a charlatan. There are episodes when the cancer that was thought to be cured swelled after the antidote was found to be a sham. The power may be within the individual. But the kindling source resides outside, in the behavior of someone else. The God belief is the greatest parental power of them all. We can isolate and optimize this behavioral operation.

There is a second good feature of the religious personality and the God Experience. The most conspicuous and immediate positive component is their powerful reinforcement value. God Experiences are potent anxiety reducers that can change human beings from trembling, incapacitated primates into confident, creative individuals.

The cumulative effects of daily uncertainties and aversive stimuli create a conditioned suppression of life in general. Operationally, the procedure is similar to certain familiar situations. If every time you go to work and begin to make suggestions the boss ridicules you, the place and the boss slowly become discriminative stimuli for response suppression. When you walk into the situation, you find yourself feeling helpless, uneasy, and incapacitated. Your spontaneity leaves and you live from day to day, dreading the next confrontation.

The average person's life is full of specific examples of conditioned suppression or learned emotional responses. If you go to class and ask questions, but the professor persistently says, "No, you're wrong," you may find silence preferable to pursual. If your husband constantly complains about the poor quality of the meals and how you don't treat him appropriately, you slip into a depressive rut from which you cannot escape. So you lose your enthusiasm for new creations and begin to eat.

As a person ages and the reinforcement history fills with multitudes of miniature aversive presentations, the anticipation generalizes to life in general. The person begins to develop a conditioned suppression for life and even for its verbal references and pictorial symbols. Every day becomes another cue for imminent disaster. The future is filled with apprehension. Conditioned suppression of life in general is also called *existential anxiety* or the anxiety of existence.

The severity of existential anxiety arises across individuals, depending on the number of conditioned suppression episodes, their duration, and their severity over a lifetime. People who have been exposed to ceaseless adversity (especially if it had large *anticipatory* components and particularly if *systematic* cues came sometime *before* the actual aversive stimulus) are prone to this disposition. The most powerful procedure involves the occurrence of the cue and the presentation of the aversive event within a variable interval or variable ratio schedule.

People who are exposed more or less continuously to intermittent anticipated punishment are paralyzed by existential anxiety. The popularity of existential philosophy after World War II was a predictable phenomenon. Millions of people, for over a decade, had been exposed to daily cues of imminent disaster. Sirens were the discriminative stimuli for anticipated destruction. As these people shuddered in bomb shelters, waiting for the death that rained down on them randomly every night, existential anxiety grew. Who would be next?

Before the war, the Great Depression had robbed them of their options for obtaining rewards and reducing the anxiety of imminent starvation, job loss, and the reclamation of their homes. Lack of money became a conditioned stimulus for the apprehension of what might come. As each neighbor in similar conditions met with bankruptcy, poverty, and social deterioration, the roots of existential philosophy grew stronger.

The acquisition of intense existential anxiety does not require the dramatic and global devastations associated with world wars or civil conflicts. Conditioned suppression of life in general can be found in any culture where the child's reinforcement history is a continuous array of anticipations of punishment. The child who waits for his father, the greater punisher, to come home day after day, also becomes a victim. If the mother threatens, "You were bad so I will tell your father," the conditioned suppression of life begins. Since the child has little capacity for understanding the trivial consequences of the task, the punishment appears as the final end to his existence.

For the child, it can take many forms: "Take care of your pet or I [the parent] will kill it"; "You were bad today so Santa Claus won't visit you"; "You wait until your father comes home and he will whip you until you bleed"; "Tomorrow I will give you a licking for what you did today." As long as one of the words or phrases in the sentence has been paired with pain or punishment ("whip," "licking") and as long as the emphasis is on the future, the conditioned suppression paradigm exists.

It's not the punishment but the *anticipation* of punishment (after a cue or stimulus) over which the child has no (or minimal) control that generates the anxiety. For example, the display of an undesirable behavior such as breaking a window and the consequent removal of an option to eat (sending a child to his or her room without dinner), although extreme, is less aversive in its consequences. In the latter situation, the punishment is delivered immediately after the behavior displayed and is clearly associated with it. As long as the conditioning is systematic, the anxiety is minimal.

Sometimes the anxiety of life becomes so intense that everything becomes aversive. Consciousness becomes a negative affect and awareness acquires the status of an aversive cue. The individual learns that a variety of behaviors can reduce this condition. Alcoholic intoxication and drug stupor are quick and easy fixes for the problem. If the intensity of the conditioned suppression increases too quickly, the responses associated with anxiety reduction may quickly become ineffective. In fact, they may become associated with negative affect; their potential positive value, because it is much much less intense than the life anxiety, is neutralized by the latter. Even God Experiences may appear diminutive. The only escape is simple self-annihilation.

Most people are not exposed to such quickly escalating schedules of anticipated aversion without some personal form of anxiety removal. It must be sufficient to begin the anxiety reduction. As the responses occur and the conditioned suppression is attenuated, they are strengthened and displayed more frequently or with greater intensity. The anxiety (in this instance, life anxiety), when it occurs, is relegated to specific times and places. Usually it is associated with times of blatant antagonism to the anxiety reduction: the death of a friend, funerals, observations of accidents, or the demise of favorite relatives.

For most of us, existential anxiety grows slowly over a lifetime. There are the occasional increases in the rate of accumulation, paired with periods of life crises (such as the 40-year mark, the time when numbers of friends and relatives die in quick succession) or with the physiological erosion that comes from repeated injuries and loss of youth. This gradual accumulation allows the occurrence of God Experiences to reduce the anxiety in a measurable amount, thus increasing their reinforcement value.

By now it should be predictable that God Experiences proliferate among normal people during times of existential crises. When loved ones die, mystical experiences can abound. The loved one appears within a few days of death; the survivor wakes to see a smiling apparition at the foot of the bed. The person hears about the wonders of the afterlife. Although it is contrived by utopian themes and cultural details (whether friends and relatives waiting across the river or long journeys into the happy hunting ground), the experiences appear real. Why only the people the person knows (out of the many billions of people who could be there) are seen, is not considered.

Religious ritual is an expected feature of the anxious intervals between the present and the great aversive stimulus of death. With each Hail Mary the anxiety is reduced. With each reading of the psalms, the anticipation is changed from the terror of the unknown to the expectation of God's rewards. Ritual allows the display of cerebellar mechanisms and removes the necessity for cerebral activity. Without it, there is minimal anticipation, and without anticipation there is no anxiety. There is also no planning for a future. Life becomes a long workday during which one must expend minimum effort until the whistle blows. Life is an interval for which one must find diversions to while away the hours, until the reward of death is given.

From a clinical perspective, which emphasizes the productivity of the individual, his or her personal stability, and a life that is relatively free of anxiety, God Experiences and religious beliefs are positive components. If a person has a healthy appraisal of himself, displays the capacity to love, engages in sexual behavior, and is spontaneous and happy, then the criteria have been met. God

Experiences, paired with their propensity to reduce existential anxiety, can be adjunct therapy.

Anxiety reduction affects more than overt behavior. Anxiety, particularly protracted anticipation, erodes the physiology of the person. Chronic anxiety produces covert changes within the body that are later mainfested in ulcers, headaches, and gastrointestinal problems. It is associated with protrusions within the lower right quadrant of the abdomen, pains across the chest, and tingling senseness down the ventral surface of the legs.

Conditioned suppression influences more than visible behaviors. Transmitters within the portions of the heart that make it beat are depleted; heart attacks have become epidemic. Blood flow is altered within particular organs; they become prone to disease and general deterioration. Muscle groups, depending on their history of individual damage and the person's lifestyle (which reflects their usage), are stretched beyond elastic limits and are irreversibly contracted. Tendons become replaced by connective tissue. The healthy human form is distorted by the cumulative effects of anxiety.

Anxiety penetrates to the level of the cell. The consequences of conditioned suppression and the maintenance of existential dilemmas inhibit the immune system. Foreign materials can proliferate within the body and the person becomes prone to flus, colds, and other social diseases. The chronically anxious person has recurrent bouts of borderline illnesses, challenged from time to time by exploratory surgery. They occur in times of great duress when the sense of self is threatened (during examination periods, promotional periods, or movement within the social group).

But the most tragic effect of anxiety is on the immune system's capacity to react to the natural peculiarities of cell division, what we commonly call *cancer*. It is an expected correlate of cell division. Considering the billions of times that cells divide and the countless trillions of possible biochemical sequences that could deviate, the existence of cancer is a necessity. No doubt there may be many initiators of these events. In addition to the spontaneous sources due to statistical accident, there are the countless carcinogens and toxic substances that can directly affect the cell's genetic potential.

The immune system can normally attack or eliminate these deviations from the genetic blueprint long before they become large enough to extend beyond the capacity to be handled. It initiates antagonistic procedures quickly, before the foreign sequences are around long enough to become habituated and recognized as a "normal" material. If the immune system is suppressed for a sufficient period of time, even the most aberrant and blatant mitotic error may be accepted. When the system returns to normal, the oddity may be ignored and allowed to grow to deadly proportions.

There are also promoters of cancer and odd cell lines. Anxiety allows their proliferation to occur. It suppresses the immune response's normal potential and allows to continue the freaks of cell division that would typically have been attacked and eradicated. After a dozen or so divisions (the time being a function of the division rate of the particular cell), the aberrant mass becomes discernible. Cells from lymphoid, breast, gonadal, and intestinal internal linking are among the fastest to divide and the most prone to odd cell division.

Recent evidence indicates that people who display religious beliefs and who report God Experiences are likely to survive for a longer period after they have been diagnosed with some forms of cancer than those who show less intense convictions. Whereas the explanation is usually ascribed to superstitious or accidental rationale, the critical consequence of relative improvement is clear. When the immunosuppression of existential terror is reduced by a belief in God and its associations, anxiety is reduced and the immune system moves toward its normal level. When the self anticipates no extinction but only a mild transformation that will last for eternity, the operation for conditioned suppression is terminated.

The effect of God Experiences and serious or deep religious beliefs on the prolongation of life of cancer patients is not very large. At present, the average extension of their life may be on the order of a few months or a year. From the individualistic perspective, quite aside from religious dogma, the survival of a human being, even for a few extra seconds, justifies the illusion. This assumes that the quality of life is maintained, that is, the person is physiologically capable of continuing the response patterns minimally defined as human behavior.

Even with God Beliefs, cancer patients ultimately die. There are occasional miracle cures, but these patients, too, die sooner or later. Most of us live our three-score and ten years, plus or minus a standard deviation. God Beliefs and religious experiences do not alter this inflexible biological fact. Indeed, it is an irony that the tenets that maintain the omnipotence of Jehovah, Allah, or the Creative Intelligence do not reveal the extension of biological time. Instead, they sublimate with extrapolations of survival into another world.

The intrinsic contradictions are not realized. If a person is cured of a disease, even if spontaneous remission rates are evident, the change is called a miracle. Religious believers praise God and the scriptures for the improvement. When each one dies within the standard deviation of 70 years, whether they are believers of this century or a thousand years ago, the demise is met with deference. The uselessness of the God Concept is avoided. If God cures with such apparent potency within a lifetime, why doesn't he extend the life of believers just a little longer? Scriptural quips do not change the mean age of mortality.

Like most behaviors that have been maintained for millenia, there is an artifact in the operation. There is some other factor that causes the behavior, but the viewer cannot or will not recognize its presence. For example, there is an old adage that "faith moves mountains." Some people take this literally or within a modern format (often imbued with the psychokinetic potential). However, faith does *not* move mountains, it only maintains the behavior that can. Behaviors produce monumental changes. Faith is merely another form of conditioned positive anticipation—it works best when the rewards have been intermittent, established by a variable interval schedule.

To explain the survival of God believers who have contracted cancer or have developed some cardiovascular disorder, a false construct is posited. What they think is the cause of the cure is not; it has been confounded by a second hidden variable that they could not measure. Neither God nor religious belief, per se, has caused the cure. Instead, the behavioral operations associated with *expectation* that God exists have reduced the anxiety of existential terror. This *reduction in anxiety* has resulted in the stimulation of the immune system and an extra few months of precious life.

Why can't the sick and desperate live longer within the framework of God belief? When one sees the hundreds of sick believers who have gone to church obediently every Sunday throughout their lives but who die before the mean, the potency of the God Belief is questioned. When one sees businessmen, struck down by stomach cancer or lymphocarcinoma, speak in contrived religious statements of poetry and prose, the discrepancy between the death and the God Belief is difficult to handle.

Often the problem lies in the timing. Close scrutiny of many subjects indicates that their religious convictions are only recent acquisitions. They appeared shortly after the diagnosis of a terminal condition. The consequent anxiety reduction from the God Belief may not be sufficient to attenuate the cumulative hidden cancers within various stages of development. They contain the aberrant cellular records of a lifetime of anxiety and stress.

We also do not know how long the temporal lobe transients paired with God Experiences could *stimulate* the immune response. There is no doubt that electrical activation of certain nuclei of the amygdala and adjacent temporal lobe can, through connections with the hypothalamus, evoke positive changes (as well) within the immune system. Antibodies can be formed against foreign substances that typically would have been ignored.

Perhaps there could be a *regression* of the immune system to previous profiles when the body was young and healthy, before it was decimated by the disease of existential crises. This regression would be analogous to "state-dependent learning." Functioning within this old context, the immune system would focus on disorders that had not been present in early ontogenetic time. Although the present immune system may have developed a tolerance to these disorders, the younger "memories" do not recognize them as a part of the "self." Consequently, the aberrant cell aggregates are attacked with renewed vigor as if they had *just* been introduced into the system. The immunological attack would begin as it should have long ago, if anxiety had not dominated.

Antibodies would be generated against the lymphoma that proliferated during the time of adolescent crises and concomitant immunosuppression. Immunofacilitation would take place to stem the aberrant growth of colon cells that divided onto their lethal course in those early years when you had only five hours of sleep per night and feared failure more than death. Lysis of cell membranes within the lungs would occur, the way it should have been done, before the existential crises of middle age and crushing responsibilities extinguished your resistance.

The answer lies within those first four years of hippocampus memory before the transformation to adult thinking. The solution is hidden within the lost images, buried within the mechanisms of adult pre-logic that dominate every human being during the first few years of life. They are the memories for which we now have amnesia. They are the memories from which the God Experience is synthesized during the TLTs, when portions of the subcortex and the synaptic matrices of infancy are momentarily merged once again. It is here that the key to the immunopotential of human survival is buried.

Admittedly, this is a bold conjecture. But if temporal lobe transients create the God Experience from old memories and synthetic combinations, why can't other forms of protein sequences be evoked as well? The relationship and multiple analogies between memory and the immune system have been pointed out before (Cunningham 1986). Both appear to depend on protein sequences for their source of storage. The innumerable combinations of amino acids within protein chains that are hundreds or thousands of units long allow myriad details of organismic history to remain. The potential is there, waiting to be tapped by the appropriate stimulus.

What is the retrieval stimulus for the immune system as it existed before the diseases of age occurred? How does one turn back the pages of cellular condition when the lymphocytes distinguished self antigens from non-self antigens? If the immunological capacity is indeed analogous to memory, then one procedure is to return the person to earlier (and healthier) contexts. The person should be re-exposed to the chemical conditions of his youth, complete with the presence or absence of allergic compounds in the air. Diets from youth should be reconsidered. The person should be returned to the hormonal conditions when life seemed unending and the future was synonymous with unlimited possibilities.

However, these would be transient and secondary operations because they are merely *associated* with the prime condition of neuronal stimulation. They may work effectively at first, as the combination of the novelty and the anxiety reduction of returning to a previous time, devoid of uncertainty, evokes a mild shift in neurochemical activity. They are conditioned stimuli and after repeated presentation without the unconditioned stimulus, their potency declines. The middle-aged man, removed from the chores of living and placed in the quiescence of his youth (amidst quiet waters and green forests), recuperates for a brief time.

Ultimately, the control for the immunological matrix exists within the brain (Stein, Schiavi, and Camerino 1976). Some series of impulses, integrated and loaded with complex information from billions of all-or-none conditions, trigger the ensemble that existed before. Like the sudden recognition of an image that inundates you with the details of how it used to be, the gates are opened and the chemical substrate is reinforced with further synthesis of the same.

The time required for the rejuvenation of the immune condition and the resurrection of the protein matrix of years is not long. If the immunological capacity parallels memory consolidation, then the duration of the experience (that starts it all again) may only be a *few seconds*. As long as the cellular consequences of the experience are maintained long enough to pass through the labile stages of electrical and chemical transformation, with minimal interference, storage could occur. Once stored, the synthesis of protein sequences, stopped many years before or suppressed by more recent antagonistic exposures, would occur again.

Evidence has accumulated that supports this possibility (Adler, 1981). Macrophages and lymphocytes have been shown to respond to neural stimulation. They may actually display the equivalence of action potentials. Components of the immune system contain receptors for the chemical transmitters that mediate communication between the nerves. Within the cellular nuclei, the immunological system contains the history of antigen challenge and antibody retaliation. Records of the protein patterns synthesized within the cell are kept. Like immunological memory banks, they wait for the appropriate sign stimulus, the particular context of neural impulses and chemical conditions, that will stimulate them once again (Besedovsky et al. 1979).

What form does immunofacilitation take? Following the TLT of the God Experience, is the immunoresponse a burst, a step, or a ramp form? If it is a step (which is highly unlikely), then the person should show improved health until some genetic clock stops or an accident eliminates a vital center of the body. If it is a ramp, then some extra amount of time must be obtained, perhaps by medical strategies, until the immune system slowly elevates to a level where it can fight the ravages of life anxieties by itself.

At present, the pattern indicates the TLT effects are pulse-like in nature. How long does the pulse last? Does it last for a few weeks or a few months or a few years? Extrapolating from clinical literature (Paul, 1984), the most likely order of magnitude involves a few weeks to a few months. Somehow, the stimulation of the TLT can enhance the immunological system, and the "miraculous" cures ensue.

But there also seems to be remission when the cancer flares again or the disease progresses to another stage of organismic degradation. This time, however, the person, psychologically at least, is ready for the end. The religious experience has been forfeited by endless ritual and religious behaviors. They have replaced the original high of the TLT. They have become symbols for that brief instant when the TLT occurred and the person knew he was special. Like all conditioned stimuli, however, they are never as powerful as the original unconditioned stimulus of the TLT. And so the second time the person dies.

Could modern medicine harness the organismic potential of TLTs? If their effects on the immune system last for a few weeks or days, could the technology be developed to stimulate the appropriate areas of the brain frequently enough for God Experiences to remain meaningful and unique and for the immune system to be maintained at the optimal level of operation? There is always the risk, if the God Experience is based on infrequency and novelty for its profundity, that it could be diminished by multiple presentations.

Imagine the potential extension of productive lives (even if the genetic barrier of 70 or so years can never be broken) if every person were to have access to this immunofacilitation. The person's body (barring genetic difficulties of protein synthesis and unusual histories of extraordinary sensitivity) could be induced to stimulate itself into a continuous state of general health. Colds, flu, and other forms of organismic challenge would be encountered and consolidated like any other environmental interaction.

The small extensions of people's lives now seen in clinical settings are symptoms of a more powerful force within each human being. Their observations are analogous to the small specks of exposure on x-ray film placed near some ugly rocks of uranium in a turn-of-the-century lab. Once the operations were specified and the critical components had been isolated, the immense power of the atom could be seen. The impossible and the unthinkable became reality. In four decades, an anomalous phenomenon was developed into the most awesome energy known.

Is there a potential within the God Experience that could lead to human cure? From these few observations, suppose analogous isolation of the procedure occurred and clarification of the mechanism were allowed? Of course, it would require the acceptance that God may not exist or that the experiences are illusionary products of the human brain. These beliefs must be challenged in order to allow the dispassionate and objective pursual of this mechanism. But if a comparable development in human potential could occur, can you imagine the power that could be used for the benefit of every human being, no matter what his or her religious or national conditioning?

Bibliography

Ader, R. 1981. *Psychoimmunology*. (New York: Academic Press).

Adler, N. 1972. The Underground Stream. (New York: Harper and Row).

Bear, D. M. 1979. Temporal lobe epilepsy: A syndrome of sensory-limbic hyperconnection. *Cortex* 15:357–84.

Bear, D. M., and P. Fedio. 1977. Quantitative analysis of interictal behavior in temporal lobe epilepsy. *Archives and Neurology* 34:454–67.

Besedovsky, H. O., A. del Ray, E. Sorkin, M. da Prada, and H. H. Keller. 1979. Immunoregulation mediated by the sympathetic nervous system. *Cellular Immunology* 48:346–55.

Browning, D. 1968. Faith and the dynamics of knowing. In *Essays in Divinity*, edited by P. Homans (Chicago, IL: University of Chicago Press), pp. 111–34.

Buckley, P. 1981. Mystical experience and schizophrenia. *Schizophrenia Bulletin* 7:516–21.

Budge, E. A. W. 1967. *The Egyptian Book of the Dead* (New York: Dover).

Clark, W. H. 1958. *The Psychology of Religion* (New York: MacMillan).

Cunningham, A. J. 1986. Information and health in the many levels of man: Towards a new and comprehensive theory of health and disease. *Advances* 3(1):32–45.

Dewhurst, K., and A. W. Beard. Sudden religious conversions in temporal lobe epilepsy. *British Journal of Psychiatry* 117:497–507.

Eleftheriou, B. E. 1972. *The Neurobiology of the Amygdala* (New York: Plenum Press).

Elhard, L. 1968. Living faith: Some contributions of the concept of ego-identity to the understanding of faith. In *Essays in Divinity*, edited by P. Homans (Chicago, IL: University of Chicago Press), pp. 135–61.

Evans-Wentz, W. Y. 1972. *The Tibetan Book of the Dead* (Oxford: Oxford University Press).

Feldman, R. G., and N. L. Paul. 1976. Identity of emotional triggers in epilepsy. *Journal of Nervous and Mental Diseases* 162:345–53.

Geschwind, N. 1983. Interictal behavioral changes in epilepsy. *Epilepsia* 24(Suppl. 1):S23–S30.

Goldensohn, E. S. 1983. Symptomatology of nonconvulsive seizures: Ictal and postictal. *Epilepsia* 24(Suppl. 1):S5–S21.

Gloor, P., A. Olivier, L. F. Quesney, F. Andermann, and S. Horowitz. 1982. The role of the limbic system in experiential phenomena of temporal lobe epilepsy. *Annals of Neurology* 12(2):129–44.

Gordon, J. E. 1967. *Handbook of Clinical and Experimental Hypnosis*. (New York: MacMillan).

Haracz, J. 1984. A neural plasticity hypothesis of schizophrenia. *Neuroscience and Biobehavioral Reviews* 8:55–71.

Harper, M., and M. Roth. 1962. Temporal lobe epilepsy and the phobic anxiety-depersonalization syndrome. Part I. A comparative study. *Comprehensive Psychiatry* 3(3):129–51.

Hergenhahn, B. R. 1982. *Theories of Learning* (Englewood Cliffs, NJ: Prentice-Hall).

Hermann, B. P., and S. Whitman. 1984. Behavioral and personality correlates of epilepsy: A review, methodological critique, and conceptual model. *Psychological Bulletin* 95:451–97.

Holland, J. G. 1981. Radical behaviorism and consciousness. In *The Metaphors of Consciousness*, edited by R. S. Valle and R. von Eckartsberg (New York: Plenum Press), pp. 97–106.

Houstan, J. P. 1986. *Fundamentals of Learning and Memory* (New York: Academic Press).

Issacson, R. L., and K. H. Pribram. 1975. *The Hippocampus. Vol. 2: Neurophysiology and Behavior* (New York: Plenum Press).

Leslie, C., ed. *Anthropology of Folk Religion* (New York: Vintage Books).

Makarec, K., and M. A. Persinger. 1985. Temporal lobe signs: Electroencephalographic validity and enhanced scores in special populations. *Perceptual and Motor Skills* 60:832–42.

Murphy, G., and L. B. Murphy. 1968. *Asian Psychology*. (New York: Basic Books).

Paul, W. 1984. *Fundamental Immunology*. (New York: Raven).

Persinger, M. A. 1980. *The Weather Matrix and Human Behavior*. (New York: Praeger).

———. 1983. Religious and mystical experiences as artifacts of temporal lobe function: A general hypothesis. *Perceptual and Motor Skills* 57:1255–62.

———. 1984a. Striking EEG profiles from single episodes of glossolalia and transcendental meditation. *Perceptual and Motor Skills* 58:127–33.

———. 1984b. People who report religious experiences may also display enhanced temporal-lobe signs. *Perceptual and Motor Skills* 58:963–75.

———. 1984c. Propensity to report paranormal experiences is correlated with temporal lobe signs. *Perceptual and Motor Skills* 59:583–86.

———. 1985. Death anxiety as a semantic conditioned suppression paradigm. *Perceptual and Motor Skills* 60:827–30.

Persinger, M. A., N. Carrey, and L. Suess. 1980. *TM and Cultmania* (Boston, MA: Christopher).

Persinger, M. A., and P. M. Valliant. 1985. Temporal lobe signs and reports of subjective paranormal experiences in a normal population: A replication. *Perceptual and Motor Skills* 60:903–9.

Peterson, E. 1966. *Psychopharmacology*. (Dubuque: W. C. Brown).

Plutchick, R., and H. Kellerman, eds. 1986. *Emotion: Theory, Research and Experience* (New York: Academic Press).

Pontius, A. A. 1984. Specific stimulus-evoked violent action in psychotic trigger reaction: A seizure-like imbalance between frontal lobe and limbic systems. *Perceptual and Motor Skills* 59:299–333.

Reiman, E. M., M. E. Raichle, F. K. Butler, P. Herscovitch, and E. Robins. 1984. A focal brain abnormality in panic disorder, a severe form of anxiety. *Nature* 310:683–85.

Reitan, R. M. and Wolfson, D. 1985. *Neuroanatomy and Neuropathology*. (Tucson: Neuropsychology Press).

Slater, E., and A. W. Beard. 1963. The schizophrenic-like psychosis of epilepsy. I. Psychiatric aspects. *British Journal of Psychiatry* 109:95–150.

Smith, A. J. 1954. *Immortality: The scientific evidence* (New York: Signet).

Spiegel, H., and D. Spiegel. 1978. *Trance and Treatment* (New York: Basic Books).

Stein, M., R. C. Schiavi, and M. Camerino. 1976. Influence of brain and behavior on the immune system. *Science* 191:435–40.

Stern, L. *The Structure and Strategies of Human Memory* (Homewood, IL: Dorsey Press).

Stevens, J., H. M. Vernon, F. Erwin, P. Pacheco, and K. Suematsu. 1969. Deep temporal stimulation in man. *Archives of Neurology* 21:157–69.

Stevens, J. R. 1982. Sleep is for seizures: A new interpretation of the role of phasic ocular events in sleep and wakefulness. In *Sleep and Epilepsy*, edited by M. B. Stern, M. N. Shouse, and P. Passouant (New York: Academic Press), pp. 249–64.

Trawick, B. B. 1963. *The Bible as Literature* (Lancaster, PA: Barnes & Noble).

Tucker, I. F. 1970. *Adjustment: Models and Mechanisms* (New York: Academic Press).

Valliant, P. V. 1982. Clinical notes from the forensic unit of a psychiatric hospital. Unpublished notes and manuscript, Laurentian University, Department of Psychology, Sudbury, Ontario.

von Eckartsberg, R. 1981. Maps of the mind. In *Metaphors of Consciousness*, edited by R. S. Valle and R. von Eckartsberg (New York: Plenum Press).

Waxman, S. G., and N. Geschwind. 1974. Hypergraphia in temporal lobe epilepsy. *Neurology* 24:629–36.

Weingarten, S. M., D. G. Cherlow, and E. Holmgren. 1977. The relationship of hallucinations to the depth structures of the temporal lobe. *Acta Neurochirurgica (Suppl.)* 24:199–216.

Index

About the Author

MICHAEL A. PERSINGER is a professor of psychology and head of the Neuroscience Research Group at Laurentian University, Sudbury, Ontario, Canada. Born in 1945, he received his Ph.D. from the University of Manitoba (1971), M. A. from the University of Tennessee (1969), and B. A. from the University of Wisconsin, Madison (1967). Dr. Persinger has published more than 100 technical articles in the areas of psychobiology, parapsychology, brain functions, and environmental health. He has also authored or co-authored six books, including *Space-Time Transients and Unusual Events* (Nelson-Hall, 1977) and the *Weather Matrix and Human Behavior* (Praeger, 1980). Dr. Persinger's major research emphasis is concerned with the clinical and experimental correlates of stimulation within the temporal lobes of the mammalian brain.